FIFTY YEARS FIGHTING

OTHER TITLES BY THE SAME AUTHOR

BY APPOINTMENT ONLY SERIES
Arthritis, Rheumatism and Psoriasis
Asthma and Bronchitis
Cancer and Leukaemia
Do Miracles Exist?
Heart and Blood Circulatory Problems
Migraine and Epilepsy
Neck and Back Problems
New Developments for MS Sufferers
Realistic Weight Control
Skin Diseases
Stomach and Bowel Disorders
Stress and Nervous Disorders
Traditional Home and Herbal Remedies
Viruses, Allergies and the Immune System

NATURE'S GIFT SERIES
Air – The Breath of Life
Body Energy
Food
Water – Healer or Poison?

WELL WOMAN SERIES
Female Cancers
Menopause
Menstrual and Pre-Menstrual Tension
Mother and Child
Pregnancy and Childbirth

JAN DE VRIES HEALTHCARE SERIES
Healing in the 21st Century
Hidden Dangers in what we Eat and Drink
How to Live a Healthy Life
Inner Harmony
My Life with Diabetes
Questions and Answers on Family Health
The Five Senses
Treating Body, Mind and Soul

NATURE'S BEST SERIES
10 Golden Rules for Good Health

THE JAN DE VRIES PHARMACY GUIDEBOOK SERIES
The Pharmacy Guide to Herbal Remedies

ALSO BY THE SAME AUTHOR
A Step at a Time (Autobiography)
Feeling Fabulous over Fifty
Life Without Arthritis – The Maori Way
Who's Next?

Fifty Years Fighting

Another Step In Time

Jan de Vries

MAINSTREAM
PUBLISHING

EDINBURGH AND LONDON

First published in Great Britain in 2004 by
MAINSTREAM PUBLISHING COMPANY (EDINBURGH) LTD
7 Albany Street
EDINBURGH EH1 3UG

ISBN 1 84018 884 7

Typeset in Garamond
Printed and bound by
Creative Print and Design, Wales

Contents

Foreword

Jan de Vries has spent much of his 67 years helping others. However, he did not choose an easy path to do so. Many will know his story well – having qualified as a pharmacist, he met the renowned Swiss naturopath Alfred Vogel and embarked upon a career in complementary medicine.

In the early days, most parts of Europe decried this form of treatment as, at best, 'cranky'. On first meeting Vogel, Jan himself expressed the view that homoeopathy was for 'old wifies' – unwittingly helping to perpetuate the stereotype.

This second volume of his three-part autobiography looks at the many struggles he has faced along the way as a practitioner of complementary medicine. Many of these still beset him and those who follow in his footsteps.

However, attitudes have undoubtedly changed. Complementary medicine is now increasingly seen to be respectable and even (to the great surprise of cynics) useful. More of those in the 'orthodox' medical profession are being won over every day.

Why is this so? There are, of course, many complex answers to this seemingly simple question. However, I believe that there is one central thread.

Orthodox medicine is focused very much on the 'illness model'. The way that illness is treated is focused on the 'problem' identified. It rarely takes into account the many influences surrounding the patient, and, crucially, getting the patient on the side of the treatment process.

Naturopaths believe that healing involves body, mind and soul, and requires the practitioner and patient to work together, in harmony, towards a positive end. One patient commented that when she saw Jan for the first time, his words were: 'Yes, we can do something about this'. No one had included her in the equation before this time.

This insight is now being shared more and more by both patients and their doctors – leading to the recognition that somewhere, somehow, what has been preached by practitioners of complementary medicine over the decades has some value.

And, much of this change in attitude has to do with the work that Jan has done during his lifetime, breaking down the barriers in the divide between complementary and orthodox medicine. One of his many gifts is as a communicator – and he uses this so very effectively in seminars, lectures, radio programmes, through articles and his books.

It is with this gift that Jan is able to help more people than those able to make their way to his clinics. Over the years, he has played a monumental role in helping to change attitudes towards complementary medicine; helping people to find a better way to manage their health; helping people to help themselves.

Jan de Vries has spent much of his 67 years helping others – helping even those he has never met.

Dr Jen Tan MB; BS
Medical Director
Bioforce (UK) Ltd

Prologue

One morning in August 1961, my three colleagues and I were all very busy, patients going in and out of our Naturopathic Clinic at Roode Wald, Nunspeet, Holland, which I had helped the Swiss naturopath Alfred Vogel to establish. It was the first of its kind in Holland. Everyone was happily going about their business when a registered letter arrived for me. It was from the Dutch Inspector of Health, who wanted to know precisely what we were doing. He was very interested in the roles of Dr Jan Kok, Dr Tine Kaayk and Dr Robert Koch, all established doctors in Holland, and also my own position as a pharmacist.

I wrote back to him clearly explaining our roles and another recorded delivery letter soon arrived summoning us to a meeting with him two weeks later. We were all very shocked by this ominous demand because we knew it could mean the end of our work at the clinic. Dr Kaayk decided not to attend but we three felt that we had nothing else to do but go. In a telephone conversation with Alfred Vogel in Switzerland he had encouraged me to stand firm, as right would always win through, and so, on a beautiful morning at the end of August, we went to Nijmegen. Everyone was rather nervous.

Being inexperienced in those days, I was in fear and trembling when we arrived at the very stately house at the Oranjesingel, Nijmegen, where the meeting was to take place. Years later, I took my family to live in that town and regularly visited the same area as it housed our bank. Every time I went there, I experienced the same feeling of dread.

The Inspector was not unfriendly but nevertheless it was a gruelling experience. He told us in no uncertain terms that we had to resign our posts in Roode Wald. I still maintain that it was the best clinic I have known in my lifetime.

He told us that there was no way for us to carry on, as the Government would not allow alternative medicine to be practised in Holland. The Inspector of Health was completely against homoeopathic and herbal medicine, stating that the methods were unproven. In addition, alternative medicine had a very bad name in Holland in those days because it held too many echoes of the Nazi era – such remedies had been popular with Hitler and his lieutenants. The Inspector insisted that we agree there and then that we would give up our posts, as it was the Government's intention to close the clinic.

In answer to Dr Koch's questions, the Inspector admitted that the world of orthodox medicine was not perfect. Doctors frequently did not have enough time for their patients, sometimes deciding what treatment a patient needed before even visiting them, and that they did make mistakes. He also admitted that many people were in hospital unnecessarily, but he remained adamant. He worked for the medical establishment who had set rules and one had to abide by those rules or face the consequences.

I asked him what the consequences would be for us if we refused to give up our positions.

He looked at me darkly and said, 'If, by tomorrow, I do not have a letter confirming your compliance with this requirement, I will have no other choice but to strip you of your right to operate as a pharmacist [I had only recently graduated] and imprison you.'

Perhaps I was naive, but I could not believe what he was saying. I looked at him again and said, 'You say that if we do not stop, we will have to go to prison?'

He replied, 'Yes, and probably for quite a long time.'

'But we are doing honest work; we only want to help people,' I exclaimed.

He merely responded that he was carrying out the law and that we would have to obey it, as our kind of medicine would not be tolerated in Holland.

I have often wondered if this man ever witnessed the growth of natural medicine. Nowadays, a third of Dutch doctors prescribe our methods and our kind of medicine. Indeed, doctors in Holland now have to study homoeopathic and herbal medicine in their curriculum and can extend their university course by an extra year to study the principles of a multi-disciplinary programme. In addition, Alfred Vogel's name became renowned in Holland and he was adored by thousands of people for his philosophies and his principles.

When we left that meeting, I was still shaking. On the drive back to Nunspeet, my two colleagues told me that they had no choice but to comply with the Inspector's demand. Dr Kok, nowadays a leading professor in medicine, then had a young family and felt he could not risk his career. Dr Koch also decided to pull back, so I was left alone. I resolved to carry on and see what would happen. I had been taught from childhood that if you do the right thing, right will always win over wrong. A miracle happened and I was left to carry on at the clinic, unimpeded.

Many times in my life I have been threatened, in the bitter fight for the freedom of choice, but thankfully, so far, I have always won!

CHAPTER ONE

My Fight for Freedom of Choice in Medicine

I have fought many battles to be allowed to practise alternative medicine. Many times throughout my 50 years fighting I have had to struggle for the freedom to choose my path. The Dutch Inspector of Health's threat in 1961 to strip me of my qualifications and send me to prison if I did not give up alternative medicine was just one of the first I have had to face.

Over the years, many different means have been tried to reduce or prevent the growth of alternative medicine and so limit freedom of choice. It is very sad that certain remedies make headway and become known and much in demand by the public only to be discredited or withdrawn from the market, apparently because they are a threat to the large drugs companies. This continues to happen worldwide.

This thought brings to mind the story of a remedy that was a blessing for many people. While I was staying in Biel, Switzerland, Professor Kazuhiko Asai sought me out in my hotel room late one evening. Professor Asai was a well-known scientist who was greatly valued in his field. He immediately got my attention by telling me that he had been diagnosed with an inoperable throat tumour. His wife, a staunch Catholic, had taken him to Lourdes, where he drank gallons of the water and also bathed in it. He then discovered that his tumour had disappeared. Because he was not a religious man, he could not believe that it was as a result of the water of Lourdes but, nevertheless, he started to investigate and found it contained a high concentration of the oxygen-giving mineral germanium. This, he felt, was the real reason for his recovery. He came to understand that germanium, which is water soluble, releases a lot of oxygen into the body. With his scientist's mind he concluded that a cancer cell is an oxygen-poor cell. As a result of this research he developed a most amazing remedy called *Germanium GE32*. Many people were involved in his trials, with no recorded side effects.

Germanium proved to be very successful, having a positive effect on the health of ME patients, cancer sufferers and patients with other degenerative diseases. Unfortunately, in the early 1990s it was discredited in the media, where it was suggested that there were side effects associated with it that had caused the death of an elderly lady, although these were never scientifically proved. Equally, I am not aware of any of my patients having had problems with *Germanium GE32*. It was a very sad day when it was taken off the market in the UK and elsewhere, leaving many people helped by this remedy with no alternative. It continues to be sold in some countries, where it is still a blessing to many. However, research is ongoing and hopefully, one day, justice will prevail and this excellent product will once again become available to those who could greatly benefit from its properties.

And what about the simple amino acid called *L-tryptophan*, a food product which was of fantastic help to insomniacs, and *Melatonin*, used to regulate sleep patterns in people with jet-lag, for example. Both were withdrawn from over-the-counter sale, as the authorities decreed that there was insufficient proof of their safety.

Then, in this very stressful world, people were not even allowed to take *Kava-kava*, a popular herbal remedy used to ease tension and calm the nerves. Was there ever any real evidence that *Kava-kava* would cause any harm? Scientifically, we can prove that anything has the capacity to kill – even drinking too much water.

It was very disappointing to see such remedies withdrawn from the market and, during my years in practice, I have been shocked to see governments use their powers to take these God-given remedies away from the people who have a right to benefit from them.

A long time ago, I gave a lecture in Germany on the subject of vitamins, minerals and trace elements, which was attended by a large number of doctors and health practitioners. After I spoke about the many benefits of these products and of the people who supplied them, I was shocked later to hear how the German police had seized the entire stock from practitioners who had used these remedies sensibly and effectively for the benefit of their patients. Where is the justice and where is the people's right to freedom of choice?

Many of these innocent remedies prescribed by practitioners, when taken in the correct dosage and following the instructions on the packet, are much safer than certain pain-killers available for sale in filling stations and supermarkets. In all my 50 years in this field, I have never heard of one single death caused by any of these natural products.

Not so long ago, my niece, a pharmacist in Holland, told me that certain homoeopathic and herbal remedies had been officially withdrawn from the market on instruction from the Government. Evidence that these remedies had helped people was not taken into consideration. I can well understand why the people who have been helped by these remedies were upset.

Despite all this legislative activity, I have seen a terrific growth in natural medicine over recent years. Homoeopathic and herbal medicines have come to the fore and slowly the public has begun to realise that if they can treat themselves with natural products, then why would they want to do so by artificial means? However, a side effect of the desire for freedom of choice was that suddenly the large drug companies began to recognise this growing trend and articles started to appear in newspapers warning of the possible deadly effects of very innocent natural remedies.

Such incidents raise a lot of questions in my mind: why are cigarettes so readily available yet each packet warns that smoking kills? Why is it possible that anyone can go into a filling station or a shop and buy as much aspirin as they like? Why is it that certain other drugs are so easily accessible in the supermarkets? With my pharmaceutical background, I cannot stress enough my deep and long-lasting concern at the way these drugs are made freely available to the public. It is the same with alcohol, which is also readily available in all manner of shops, making it possible for people to drink themselves to death.

Where is the evidence that natural remedies ever killed anybody, compared to the thousands of people who are killed by the use of tobacco and alcohol?

The explosion of pharmaceutical drugs has been a worry for me ever since I qualified as a pharmacist in 1958. One question concerned me from the start: where does medicine go from here? I looked at the vast and growing numbers of sleeping tablets, tranquillisers, antibiotics and long-term drugs on the market, and asked myself, 'Is there not another answer to this?'

Later, when hormonal products were developed and hormone replacement therapy (HRT) was thought to be the great new discovery of the age, I was horrified to realise that this treatment, devised to alleviate severe menopausal symptoms, was being used by some women purely to stop the development of facial wrinkles. From the start, I was deeply concerned about the potential side effects of HRT and lobbied against its use, but nobody believed me. I caused much anger in the orthodox world simply by pointing out that there are so many alternatives in nature, which do exactly the same as HRT, that we should be encouraging women to take the alternative, healthier route.

My concern increased as I found myself treating patients on HRT who were suffering from phlebitis, thrombosis and breast cancer. Still this was not enough to convince the medical profession that HRT was not the miracle they had assumed. I felt alone in the wilderness, where people thought I had gone completely cranky when I preached about the effects of this unnatural approach. It was not until recent confirmation of an increase in breast cancer in patients taking hormone replacement therapy that people started to listen.

Another battle involved a certain sleeping tablet that I knew to have serious side effects. I pleaded repeatedly with the Pharmaceutical Society to take this tablet off the market. When I heard from two Dutch ladies visiting my Troon clinic that that particular sleeping tablet appeared to have resulted in many suicides in Holland, I again appealed to the Society to investigate that drug, but to no avail as trials had shown that it was safe. Another ten years elapsed, during which this medication claimed even more victims. It was only when concerns were raised through the media that the situation came to a head and it was withdrawn from sale.

Some time ago, a tall, handsome gentleman came to see me. He was known in water sports circles as an excellent canoeist. He had been very unwell for three weeks and his skin was completely yellow. He told me his doctors were at a loss. I discovered that he had been taking a certain drug for the treatment of fungal infections that I had been fighting against for many years. It was this which had adversely affected him and in particular his liver. I gave him Alfred Vogel's *Milk Thistle Complex, Hepar Sulph* and *Echinaforce* along with a strict liver diet. Fortunately, these remedies helped to restore his health and he continues to be one of the top sportsmen in his field. He wrote to the drug company and to the medical establishment about his concerns, all to no avail. The reply he received was that his symptoms were listed in the leaflet detailing contraindications. It is very unfortunate that this same drug is still being prescribed. We have both tried to fight against this drug, even writing to the newspapers, but it was all ignored. It was claimed that the drug had been tried and tested, and that nobody would die from taking it. However, I must confess that this fellow was very near to death, and his wife and myself had to work hard to keep him alive and get him back to normal.

Again I would stress that in all these 50 years of practising alternative medicine, I have never known of one single death attributed to the use of natural remedies. We have, however, seen many with so-called medicinal drugs. Fifty years ago, when my fight began, it was claimed that herbal medicine was of no benefit. Today remedies like *Kava-kava* are banned in Europe while the Irish Government has made *St John's Wort* and *Ginkgo biloba* prescription only, giving people the false impression that these remedies are harmful. Was that ever proven? Was there ever a case where those remedies did any harm if taken in the right quantity and by following the instructions? When the public does not adhere to the specified dosage, or exaggerates the advice given on the container, this is when problems may possibly occur.

A question mark is raised every time there is a challenge to natural remedies, when the orthodox world says there is not enough evidence that they work while on the other hand saying that they can cause death or disease! I have never experienced either outcome with the thousands of people I have treated. Certainly, orthodox medicine costs a vast amount of money and obtains all the necessary grants to prove itself, yet even after spending huge sums of money on research, usage can show that they are not as safe as first thought. Perhaps if similar funding was available to alternative remedies, we would finally be able to lay these misunderstandings to rest.

In nature, everything is in harmony, and it is only when Man disturbs this harmony of Creation that problems arise. This was clearly illustrated by sheep belonging to my colleague and mentor, Alfred Vogel. One night they escaped from their field into his walled herb garden. Here Vogel grew many herbs and, in his methodical way, he had separated all the poisonous plants – such as digitalis, belladonna (also known as deadly nightshade), aconite and many others – from the non-poisonous ones. When Vogel found the sheep in the garden the following morning, he discovered to his horror that they had eaten their way through all his herbs. Yet not a single sheep died, as one plant had counteracted the effects of another.

Are natural remedies dangerous? No. It would take a large amount of a natural remedy to kill a patient. If we go about things intelligently, we can use these God-given methods and remedies for the benefit of all. One has to know what one is doing and that is the reason education is so important. Practice and experience are essential if we are to move forward.

Sometimes, when I see medical authorities, with the help of the police, going around as biblical 'breathing lions', I feel that we live in a police state rather than a democracy, where people have lost the right to choose for themselves. I saw this clearly not long ago when two official, well-dressed gentlemen entered a health food store, poked around and finally examined one single tube of ointment. There was an illegal medicinal claim on that tube, so they immediately asked to see the owner. Using their powers, they warned him that if he did not remove this product from his shelves immediately, he would be prosecuted.

This reminded me of a situation in which I was once involved. This was at a meeting about a particular natural medicine, which was attended by the Secretary of State for Health, health officials and a number of others who were invited by a very good friend of mine. This lengthy, difficult meeting had been arranged in order to try to gain some recognition for various natural medicines. Throughout the meeting, a gentleman in a smart, tailored suit sat silently in the corner. At the end of the meeting, my friend asked to be introduced. He persisted in asking this man what his job was, until it was eventually revealed that he was the president of a large pharmaceutical company. My friend realised then just how much the growth of natural medicine is influenced by the powers of outside organisations.

Some years ago, I was asked to do a series of lectures at the

Bastyr University in Seattle in the United States, where people are trained in natural medicine. One particular morning, I spoke to the students about our identity as practitioners. I told them that they should be very proud of the profession that they had chosen. The founder of the university, Dr John Bastyr, was present that morning and, after the lecture, he told me that he could wholeheartedly identify with every word I had said. He agreed that we should indeed be proud of our identity as people who had learned to understand the needs of others and who wanted to help them using alternative methods, but, he said, it is a bitter fight. It is very sad how much opposition can be caused when certain therapies and natural medicines are found to benefit people. In order to learn to know one's identity, one has to face many character-forming experiences, but the path is not an easy one, as I have realised over the past 50 years.

From Seattle I went to another university in Portland, Oregon, and gave a similar lecture on identity. Amongst the many people present was a young man who had trained in orthodox medicine. He was of Scottish origin, so I had a nice talk with him. As we parted, he looked at me and said, 'I am going to fight to win recognition for alternative medicine' and fight he did. When I see the work that he is doing today, the things that he has achieved and the methods he has established, I am very happy that I was part of the reason he became involved in alternative medicine. I told him that whatever he did, if he did his job honestly and worked towards freedom of choice, he would be able to help people. It was a hard fight for him but, nevertheless, he won through and he has been very successful, becoming a well-known and respected practitioner.

I also remember the struggle for recognition experienced by an excellent Dutch GP, Dr Moerman, many years ago. He had known the sadness of cancer in his own family and started to look for an answer. He kept carrier pigeons and wondered to himself, 'Why don't my pigeons have cancer?' He studied the life of pigeons to the full – their diet, the amount of oxygen that they inhaled in flight, everything about them – and finally came to the conclusion that it must be due to their diet.

Using this knowledge, he proceeded to develop a particular diet for human cancer sufferers with the addition of some vitamins, minerals and trace elements. Dr Moerman helped many people using this diet, but he received no recognition for his achievements. In fact, the medical establishment made it so difficult for him that he sometimes thought of giving up. However, with the help of some others – let us call them 'Moerman doctors' – his fight for acceptance began. It took well over ten years to prove his findings, but, with help and financial support, he finally received the recognition he deserved from the Dutch Government. He had helped so many people and, through this research, it was established that cancer was a metabolic disease. This was a very helpful study that has been of great benefit to many people.

The struggle is not always solely with the authorities. Regrettably, professional jealousy can also rear its head at times. I have never understood the reason for this, as I believe that we should love our neighbour as ourselves, especially in medicine where we have made the decision to help people.

Jealousy could have destroyed a very famous Dutch herbalist who had tremendous knowledge in this field. People went to him by the busload just to get a few minutes of his time. My mother took my little sister, who was born with a cancerous tumour, to him and, even though I was very young, I could see how much she improved. He was a great help to many people and he only prescribed mixtures of herbs which he had formulated. I have never heard of anyone dying from his treatments.

Orthodox practitioners resented his popularity. Soon, he started receiving letter after letter from the authorities demanding that he stop his practice. Even the threat of imprisonment did not prevent him continuing with his good work. He said, 'I am working for an honest cause. I want to help people. I want to make them better, and I cannot see that I am doing anything wrong.' After a number of warnings, the police came, handcuffed him and put him into prison. From there, he wrote that he was happy to be imprisoned if it meant that people would one day have the freedom to make their own choice as to how they wanted to be treated. He was detained in prison for a number of weeks, then released with a warning that he could not practise herbal medicine.

He ignored this warning and found a way to start in practice again. He brought an orthodox doctor into his practice, who first examined the patients and took their blood pressure before he himself treated them. Thus the authorities were able to turn a blind eye and he continued in practice for many years thereafter. His tenacity again showed that right will always win over wrong. To the day he died, he practised what he believed in – helping other people.

One way to help is simply to listen, even to the little things that someone has to say. Listening is a very great art and one we all need to learn. This brings to mind a case that made quite a stir in its day. It involved a Dutch gentleman of very impressive appearance. Whenever he was consulting, the streets around his house were filled with cars even though no one could quite explain exactly what he did. Sadly, when one old lady who went to him died – not as it transpired from his ministrations but from a combination of age and disease – her family took legal action against him. Witnesses were called from both the orthodox and the alternative fields, and I was asked to speak on his behalf as an expert in alternative treatments.

Everybody who was involved took the case very seriously but no one could find any evidence that he had done anything wrong. When I asked him what he did with his patients, he had one simple answer. 'I am only a listener. I am a good listener, and I give as good advice as I can. I have never taken anybody off medication they have been prescribed by their doctors, nor have I advised them to stop taking it. I have only given them advice for natural living.' This major case was a complete waste of money, because all that this good man did was listen to people's needs. Today, we have forgotten how to listen to the needs of others, particularly patients who seek help with the problems that are making their lives so miserable.

When I think of the misunderstandings and problems

encountered, and the struggle to attain recognition for alternative medicine, I again ask myself, 'Where is the freedom of choice?' Bickering does not help people. After all, natural medicine is as much aimed at alleviating human suffering as orthodox medicine. Both groups of practitioners have chosen to help people in need. So why don't they get together to help people and end this ruthless attitude of withdrawing remedies that are known to be of benefit? The drive towards ever-greater profits must be put aside in favour of the only worthy motive: striving with all our hearts to help people in need.

I had occasion to lecture on freedom of choice many years ago in Toronto, which boasts the largest education centre for natural medicine in Canada. What a wonderful spirit was present, especially amongst the younger college students who wanted to fight for their profession, to understand their role and to work towards something that they believed in.

Two years later, when I lectured at the same college, a young fellow came to me and said, 'Do you remember two years ago when you spoke on the identity of the practitioner?' He continued, 'I was not a student. My friend had brought me to listen to you.' He said that he had been contemplating buying a photography shop, as he was a qualified photographer. However, the night after the lecture he could not sleep. He thought of all the things I had said about alternative medicine and realised that he had become interested in the field. The following day, he returned to the college and enrolled on a course of study to become a natural health practitioner. Today, he is one of the most successful practitioners in Canada, and for one simple reason – he did it from the heart. Only if we put our heart and soul into this work can we be successful.

Freedom of choice in medicine will be a wonderful thing, but we must go about achieving it with common sense and intelligence. People must be educated to make the right choices in what they eat and drink, and how they exercise. It is a major task to educate thousands of people on the dangers involved when they daily buy a packet of cigarettes, or drink too much alcohol, or go into a shop or filling station for paracetamol or other drugs. Let's be honest with each other and then we can help this world more effectively and help people to attain better health.

CHAPTER TWO

My Fight against Degenerative Diseases

Just imagine the Underground in London on a Monday morning at around quarter past seven, when the congestion charge had just been put into operation and commuters were packed into the Tube like sardines. Imagine that confined, bacteria-filled space, some people coughing, some looking very ill, and imagine having to be part of that journey for sometimes an hour or more. One can imagine what effect this could have on the immune system. I boarded that Tube at Marylebone on the way to my Hadley Wood clinic, my last stop being Cockfosters. After a little while, I was able to get a seat. Next to me sat a fairly plump young lady with a child on her lap, both of whom looked very ill. This did not surprise me, as I saw the rubbish the mother was eating, while the child was obviously addicted to the nasty-looking coloured sweets that she popped into her mouth one after the other.

It was not long before the mother started to moan and groan. She rubbed her legs, stood up and was clearly in a lot of pain. Hearing her mother's distress, the child started to cry. It was a very difficult scene. Then, unusually for the Tube, she plucked up the courage to speak to me. She described the terrible pain she was experiencing. I could see from her joints that, young as she was, she was suffering from arthritis, which must have given her a lot of discomfort. I asked her what she would like me to do about it. She answered, 'You can help me. You are the television doctor – I have seen you many times. So, please, give me some advice.'

I felt very sorry for this mother and her child. When people ask for my help, I try to offer what advice I can. It is my vocation. I started to question her about her daily diet, which I soon realised was appalling. The problems ranged from very irregular meal times to the type of food that she was eating. In this way, she had introduced toxins into her system, which had slowly affected her blood, resulting in the pain she was now experiencing. The body will cry out for help when it is not being treated properly. I started to tell her all about a natural wholefood diet and what steps she could take to change her lifestyle. I also told her that I was concerned about her child. One could see from the girl's behaviour that there were problems that desperately needed attention. She was almost uncontrollable, to my mind because of the amount of sugar that she had consumed during that short space of time, and the artificial colouring in those sweets was very detrimental to the child's health. I asked the mother how much sleep her daughter got and if she was a happy child. She told of a life where money was tight and of much unhappiness since her husband walked out to be with someone else. It was not a happy scene to start off a Monday morning but, nevertheless, she showed a willingness to listen. When we arrived at Finsbury Park, where she was due to get off, she asked if she could join me to my destination, as she wanted to talk further. So, as we continued to Cockfosters, I wrote out some simple dietary tips for her and her daughter, and arranged to send her Alfred Vogel's *Knotgrass Complex* and *Devil's Claw*, along with *Flaxseed Oil* to be taken at bedtime. I am so happy to say that with this help, possibly coupled by reading several of my books, including *Realistic Weight Control*, this lady began to take an interest in looking after herself responsibly and was able to reduce her weight. She wrote to me enclosing a photo of her child, who looked much happier. Her hyperactive tendencies, which were heading in a very negative direction, had reduced due to many changes to her diet, as well as taking *Child Essence*, which I had also advised.

I am not planning in this chapter to discuss at length dietary management or even lifestyle. In my many books, I have already covered this topic in great depth. However, I do want to say that over the years I have been in practice, I have seen the increase of many degenerative diseases and seen how these particular diseases are often misunderstood. Where did it all start?

By observing those commuters on that London Tube, we get an idea where things are going wrong, beginning possibly as far back as when they were young children, with childhood illnesses perhaps neglected or treated improperly. I touch on this in my book *Mother and Child.*

If we start to adopt an unhealthy lifestyle, we are just inviting more problems. The body is a wonderful device that tells us if something goes wrong. When children cannot sleep, are hyperactive or under par, it is all too easy to say things will turn out all right if we just give it time. However, it is essential to put things right at the time. We must look sensibly at our lifestyle when we realise that something is wrong. A willingness to listen and to make any necessary changes is very important, as can be seen with the lady on the Tube. She was willing to listen, willing to follow my advice and thus she leads a totally different life today. In her last letter, she told me how happy she now is and that she has a nice man in her life.

We cannot get away from the fact that our bodies are constantly under attack. Through the food and drink that we consume, we can come into contact with many chemicals and additives that are not good for us and, if we do not take appropriate precautions, we can lay our bodies open to problems.

I have often said that in suppressing disease, we create a nation of invalids. I saw that clearly in a patient who arrived at my clinic in a wheelchair. Two years earlier, he had been diagnosed with multiple sclerosis (MS). This is a degenerative disease that can often cripple one for life. I carried out a test on him and, on noticing he had nicotine poisoning, advised him that he must stop smoking. I explained the Roger MacDougall diet to him in depth and offered him advice about adopting a healthier lifestyle. Using a Dutch saying, I told him, 'It is not five minutes to twelve, it is five minutes past twelve.' In short, he must take action now. If he did not stop smoking immediately, his health would deteriorate to such an extent that the MS would cripple him for life. Fortunately, he followed my advice and his health slowly improved.

Let there be no misunderstanding – one cannot cure multiple sclerosis, but one can control it. I have often seen with smokers that nicotine has a terrific influence on the myelin sheaths, causing them to break or release their deposits and, thereafter, signs of MS will probably appear. That was the case with this young man. He made great improvements and carried out my instructions to the letter, until he had a major row with his girlfriend, which ended their romance.

He was so devastated by this that he started smoking again. I did not see him for a long time afterwards, until that day he arrived in his wheelchair and, in tears, told me what had happened. He asked, 'What can I do? I am now completely wheelchair-bound. Is it too late?'

Very often, once the damage is done, one can do very little. Sadly, in this case a lot of symptoms associated with MS were already apparent, like double vision, lack of bladder control, pins and needles, and little or no feeling in his feet. I felt sorry for this young man. All too often the spirit is willing, but the flesh is weak and, especially when a traumatic event occurs, the tendency is to give up, which is entirely the wrong thing to do. This always disappoints me greatly, and I feel so powerless to get the message over to the patient. It is vital not to give up when this sort of thing happens.

On the other hand, I am often encouraged. Some years ago a young, very pretty woman struggled into my clinic to see me. She told me that she had an executive post at one of the large banks, but, at the height of her career, was stricken with MS. The doctor had told her that she should give up her job as her MS was progressing. She was also quite well known in horse riding circles and found her illness was restricting her activity in this area too. She also told me she was on the verge of getting married and really wanted a child.

I looked at this charming young lady and told her that she must be very positive – that together we would positively handle this and positively we would do what we could for her. I could see from the determination in her eyes that she was prepared to do what was necessary. At that stage, she could hardly walk down the stairs and, in fact, she had suffered some bad falls. I could fully understand why the doctor had advised her to give up her work.

Although I usually agree with doctors, in this case I felt she should remain in her job. I asked her if she was willing to follow a sensible diet and if she was prepared to do all I advised. She nodded that she was, saying she would do everything possible. So she went on a strict gluten-free diet and I gave her a course of injections. These measures, together with monthly visits to the clinic, helped her to continue working. Her health gradually improved and, as I write, she is in remission, able to do anything she wishes. Her job was her salvation because it helped to keep her mind off her illness. She was also able to continue horse riding, which was a great comfort to her.

Her future husband was also most supportive. Once she was able to control the MS, they got married and they have a lovely daughter. She was so eager to adhere to all my recommendations that she even devised a lot of recipes that can be found in my book *New Developments for MS Sufferers*. In that book, she also relates a little of her own story. It is very important to realise that, with sensible advice and determination, one can often go a long way to improve one's own health.

We see this so often with cancer patients. This is another degenerative disease, which I often call 'a monster', yet with determination, one can do so much. I have helped many people – including some of my own family – through the trauma of cancer. I have also seen that by using that determination in not accepting cancer, one can do a great deal.

I was greatly encouraged by a man who came to me, having been told by his doctor that he had two months to live. He had prostate cancer, which unfortunately had spread. When I first saw this gentleman, he was very yellow and extremely tired, but he said that he could not accept his prognosis. He told me he had a wonderful wife and family, and he wanted to live longer. One can often do a lot to help oneself if one refuses to accept that nothing can be done and is determined to fight. I have fought many battles with people in this same condition. Victory is not always possible, but there are many who succeed. As I have often said, a cancer cell is like a brain cell. Visualisation and positive action are often of great benefit, and such was the case with this man. I told him that

I felt there was probably some hope for him. I also told him that he should eat organic foods and that there were certain foods he must avoid, as I had established he had some allergy problems.

One has to treat each cancer patient as an individual. Even if there are 60 patients with prostate cancer, 60 with stomach cancer or 60 with lung cancer, every patient is different, and the problem has to be tackled individually, as so many characteristics, as well as the background to each illness, have to be taken into account in each situation.

The gentleman's wife later told me that he went home and thought about what I had said. The next day, she saw him digging up part of their beautiful lawn. He screened it off, fertilised it with natural substances and told his wife that he was going to grow his own vegetables and fruit. Fortunately, he had the strength to carry out this work and it also helped to take his mind off his problems. He worked hard and got the whole plot ready to grow fresh organic foods.

Seven years later, he looked a picture of health. With a smile, he said, 'My doctors are so happy with me. They don't know what has happened. I have to do a testimonial for the hospital.' He said he was delighted that he felt so well and would welcome my help in keeping it that way. He told me that his organic gardening had become of great interest to him. Just the day before, he had picked some of his broad beans and, an hour later, his wife had used them when cooking lunch. One could not eat vegetables that were fresher or that tasted better than that. He enthused about the enjoyment they got from the vegetables and the help he was able to give other growers. Most important of all, he said, 'I am alive and kicking, and, even at my age, can do what I like.' He beamed with happiness because he had achieved something in life, he had proved others wrong and had seen for himself what he could do to help himself to better health.

This is often the secret of the whole matter. I have seen it with other similar cases. One young girl particularly comes to my mind. She had developed a nasty ovarian cancer while studying hard. She was very determined to achieve her goal, but sadly, in the middle of her studies, she was faced with this tremendous conflict. Luckily, she was quite philosophical about it, saying she wanted to do the very best she could. I explained to her that the best thing was for her to back up everything that her oncologist advised with good dietary management and cancer-fighting supplements. Luckily, she did not need an operation and the specialists had agreed that she could benefit from some supportive complementary treatment.

I often describe cancer as being like a war: a battle between degenerative cells and regenerative cells. We often see with chemotherapy or radiotherapy that both types of cells are killed. So it is best to be positive and help with good dietary management and remedies to build up the army of regenerative cells in order to achieve victory over the degenerative cells. During our discussions, I told her of the tremendous findings of Professor Shamsuddin who, after years of research, found a wonderful protein, *IP-6* and *inositol*, on the inner wall of a grain of rice. Having isolated that protein, he found that he would probably be able to control cancer cells. After all, cancer is a condition in which cells are out of control.

This young lady was as eager to tackle this disease as she was in her studies. I was delighted by her attitude. I have often noted that, in the fight against degenerative diseases, the more positive one is, the better, and the more one wants to fight, the better. It was most encouraging to see this young patient go from strength to strength by fighting her way through. She even managed to continue her studies and, I am delighted to say, she has been successful in her battle.

CHAPTER THREE

My Fight against the Media

While I was contemplating this chapter, something happened that I will touch on later, which made me aware of just how influential the media can be. They can have a powerful impact on one's life, both negative and positive, with enormous implications for the present and the future, as indeed can any form of publicity.

While I was pondering this particular subject, a hairdresser came into my consulting room. I recognised his name as being very well known in his field and I have several patients who speak highly of him. I listened as he explained why he had finally decided to consult me with what appeared to be an incurable neck problem. Through his profession he had obviously put a lot of strain on his neck, which had led to restrictions in that area. X-rays revealed that he had severe cervical spondylitis.

Several of his customers had recommended me, but he was basically scared to let anyone touch his neck which, in principle, is a very sensible attitude as many mistakes can be made while treating neck problems. He asked an orthopaedic surgeon, a regular customer at his salon, what his thoughts were on alternative medicine. The surgeon asked him who he was planning to consult. When he replied, 'Jan de Vries', the surgeon said, 'Well, my advice to you is that if you have too much money, you go to him and he will certainly help you to get rid of it.' The hairdresser responded that many of his customers spoke highly of me and said my fees were very reasonable. The surgeon said it was up to him.

A few days later, another well-known consultant was in his salon, so he sought his advice. He said, 'These people do not know what they are doing. I would be very careful.' To this, the hairdresser said that he knew I had been in practice for a great number of years, so I probably did know what I was doing. Because of the conflicting reports, and not being satisfied with what he had heard, the hairdresser went to his own doctor and asked for his opinion. The doctor said, 'Well, if we can't help you, you should perhaps give him a try. I have heard about him and know that he has been in practice a long time.' At least this comment was unbiased.

When negative things are said, either publicly or in the media, they often come from people who have little or no knowledge of alternative medicine. Luckily, an editor from one of the major newspapers came into his salon. The hairdresser asked him what he thought. The editor spoke of me in glowing terms, told him that he had heard from so many people that I had helped them and advised that he should see me without delay. Based on that very positive report, the hairdresser came to see me. I helped him with acupuncture and soft-tissue manipulation, and prescribed Alfred Vogel's *Knotgrass Complex* and *Devil's Claw*. He now tries to convert the orthodox people who, he said, were probably only jealous because they had heard of some of my successes with patients they were unable to help.

It is often very difficult, even through the media, to make known what one is capable of until the proof is visible. Through the media and lectures, I have often shown what my work can achieve and how the results have proved a blessing to so many people. Positive publicity is wonderful and very often it comes through word of mouth – from people who have been for treatment and been helped who then tell others. I love to treat hairdressers because, if their treatment is successful, they will let their many customers know.

Nevertheless, I have had some serious fights with the media, often caused by jealousy or ignorance. The incident I touched on at the start of this chapter occurred when I was asked by a university to lecture to a group of some 500 experienced nutritionists and alternative therapists who were attending a congress. Everyone listened attentively to all I had to say and asked some very thought-provoking and stimulating questions. However, towards the end of the questioning, a group of people from the media – obviously totally against alternative medicine – started asking me some very awkward questions, which I believe I answered adequately.

They were obviously there to criticise alternative medicine and stated that there was no proof that alternative medicine worked. I responded that one cannot argue with results and that a number of universities nowadays are producing evidence to show that it does work. They also claimed that homoeopathy was useless, whereupon I told them that at the University of Utrecht, Holland, it had been shown that even the lowest potency of homoeopathy still changed cells.

Not satisfied with my answers, the inevitable happened. The local newspaper published an article stating that alternative medicine did not work. This was widely read and discussed, causing some very negative feedback. I phoned the reporter and asked if she would retract her comments, offering to send her evidence to show that it does work. I also advised her to speak to several specialists in this field who would corroborate what I had said. I told her that orthodox medicine was not always successful, and that it is fortunate enough to receive all the funding needed for research, whereas alternative medicine has had to prove itself by the successes gained with the patients themselves. The voice of the patients speaks loud enough to show that it does work. Fortunately, the reporter did retract her comments.

Alternative practitioners do their best to help with human suffering using remedies that have few side effects. On the other hand, we are often shocked when we hear of the contraindications of drugs. While writing this chapter, I was reminded of the time I got into deep trouble when Gloria Hunniford and I spoke on air on the subject of HRT. All I said was that, in the many years I had been in practice, I had never seen any side effects when using alternative remedies to treat the symptoms of the menopause and that I would gladly recommend them. I had, however, observed cases of thrombosis, phlebitis and breast cancer in patients who were prescribed HRT. So why not treat these troublesome menopausal symptoms with natural remedies? As we are natural beings, we should use a natural approach. I reiterated that I had seen many side effects with the use of orthodox medicine during the years I had been in practice.

This caused trouble with the medical authorities and I was asked to retract that statement, which I refused to do, because I was absolutely certain that I was right. Many years later, national and international newspapers, television and radio have now verified my comments. It is still an irrefutable fact that we are born in nature, we belong to nature and we have to obey the laws of nature, which will only benefit us.

On another occasion, I got into quite a bit of trouble with the British Federation of Pig Breeders, who lodged a serious complaint against me. They had followed some of my BBC radio broadcasts and had become extremely annoyed about my criticisms of the poor pig, telling people not to eat pork, sausages, bacon, ham or gammon. They took these remarks very seriously and I was informed that legal action would follow. One of the top people from the BBC asked to see me to discuss what they should do about it. I told them that there was not a soul in the world who can contradict the fact that the pig contains very high levels of animal acid and animal fat, which I have found to be detrimental to sufferers of rheumatism or arthritis. He asked me to clarify that fact on subsequent programmes, which I duly did. I made it clear to everyone that the pig may be a very nice and intelligent animal, but that its meat is very acidic and has a very high fat content. Therefore, if people have had problems of acidity during their lives, then they would probably benefit from eliminating pork from their diet. That is the only reason I often speak against the pig. Fortunately, no more was heard about that particular incident.

Another situation comes very clearly to my mind. At the time I had a regular and successful slot on the ITV programme *This Morning*, and I was asked to demonstrate methods of manipulation that I had found to be greatly successful. Someone – who I can only think was very jealous – played a very dirty trick. This person managed to get a letterhead from *This Morning*, wrote a letter to me and signed it from the researcher. In it he stated that my methods were totally unacceptable, that I would no longer be required to appear on the programme and that I would probably get into trouble because of the claims I had made. I was mystified because everybody seemed to be very happy with what I had done, so I went to see the researcher and showed her the letter. She immediately said that it was a fake, that it was completely untrue, that nobody there had ever written such a letter and that I would be on as normal the next time I was due to appear. This demonstrates the desperate lengths some people will go to when they are consumed with jealousy. I decided to ignore the whole situation as I thought it was not only childish, but that it would make no sense to take it further. Sadly, I have become used to such situations, which can occur when one is in the public eye. One day, this particular character will have to deal with the consequences of his actions, because one justice in life still prevails: you reap what you sow.

Now another battle looms large, which is being fought at least in part by the media. Although there have been many battles to promote the benefits of natural medicine and many criticisms of it made by the media, there has also been tremendously positive coverage. However, powers at work against natural medicine are now using other methods too. Potential EEC legislation seems determined to deprive the public of their right to much that is good in natural medicine, with medicine control agencies having the task of trying to withdraw remedies from the market, even though they have been available and beneficial to the public for many years. Remedies such as *Kava-kava, St John's Wort, Ginkgo biloba, L-tryptophan* and many others have already come under attack. When a friend of mine received a visit from two gentlemen who told him to remove certain remedies from his shelves, he asked, 'Have we landed in a police state? Do people have freedom of choice or is this all coming to an end?' How appropriate this question appears to be.

There appears to be considerably more interference than ever before, often from people who have limited knowledge, resulting in even trained and experienced practitioners in established practices being refused the recognition they deserve.

In the 50 years that I have been working in this field, I never believed that we would be up against such barriers. At an exhibition, television was used, perhaps unwittingly, to brand a product which many people had found useful as useless and expensive. Something that I have long fought against are the high prices that practitioners sometimes charge – the enormous charges made to the public for some remedies that cost so little to manufacture. However, that occurs not only in alternative medicine, but in orthodox medicine too. If we investigate the prices being charged for alternative remedies, then it would be only fair that the media compare both sides, as there are so many orthodox remedies on the market that are far too expensive in comparison to what it costs to produce them.

It is very sad that in the 50 years that I have been in practice, we have learned so very little from the past. Restrictions, rules and regulations are all necessary. One cannot oversee such a big field without disciplines and regulations, but what I have fought for during these 50 years is justice, freedom of choice and a melding together of the two principles that can often be combined to benefit the patients. I often get calls from a hospital or a doctor asking me what course I am following with a particular patient and, at such times, I am more than happy to explain what I am doing because the patient deserves the attention and cooperation to get better. So much could be done if all this bigotry and drive for profit was put aside and the patients were put first. During lectures, I always tell students that this is the most important thing we can ever do. It is this freedom I want from the media.

It saddens me so much when, in order to make a shocking

story that would catch the attention of the public, a journalist will set out to strip away all the positive aspects of alternative medicine and twist the facts to suit himself. This is often the problem today – not only in alternative medicine but in all situations of life where, for their own advantage, newspapers often sensationalise articles to excite or shock the public. It is sad to see how little we have learned from the many mistakes that have been made in the past. However, we must hold on to the belief that right will always win over wrong. I often think that those people who tell lies are probably just out to shock the public, or have probably been set up. Such people will not benefit from their actions.

Overall, I have been very lucky with the media and they have not been too hard on me. On the positive side, I have had a lot of wonderful testimonials published in newspapers and magazines. I remember being packed out with patients after a young Celtic footballer mentioned visiting me in an interview with one of the main national papers. His doctor had told him he would never play again, but after two treatments from me he was playing better than ever and is still playing today. Such comments are always very welcome and much appreciated. I was very pleased that this young footballer did as I advised, following my instructions to the last detail.

The positive side of the media is quite encouraging, especially as they cannot deny the fact that many people who have been disappointed in their regular treatments and who have sought refuge in alternative medicine have benefited to the extent that they have progressed from a very handicapped life to a very happy situation. One cannot argue with the results in such cases, which do much to highlight the success of natural medicine. I will continue to ask why, if we can treat health problems naturally, should we do it artificially? We are born in nature, we belong to nature and we have to obey the laws of nature in order to be in harmony with our Creator and ourselves.

CHAPTER FOUR

My Fight against Addictions Today

I am often labelled as addicted to writing books. Whilst I would disagree with that statement, I confess to being addicted to my work, for one very simple reason. When I was about 17 or 18 years old, I was both studying at university and working extremely hard in a pharmacy at the weekends to earn some money. At that time, I started my fight for something I thought would not only be beneficial to those with addictions but also something that was needed by society at that time.

One particular day, a man about my age came into the pharmacy and called me over. He told me about his terrific struggle against drug addiction and how he was unable to beat it. Around that time, various addictive drugs from the Far East were becoming more available in Holland, attracting interest mainly from the younger generation. This fellow had become involved with a girl who was addicted to cannabis. As he was very much in love with her, he wanted to please her and, in so doing, he started to experiment with drugs, getting mixed up in the drug scene. In the then non-permissive society in which we lived, drug addicts faced a tremendous struggle, and only limited help and understanding was available to people in their predicament. During our conversation, I became aware that, although this problem was not perceived as serious in Holland at that time, a lot of young people were being drawn into this increasing drug culture. When I realised the struggles they faced and the associated problems, it only reinforced my commitment to health. I started to fight to improve the health and well-being of addicts and to achieve a better quality of life for them and for all those still affected by all the struggles and deprivation of the Second World War.

When I investigated the whole issue of soft and hard drugs, I was amazed at what I learned and I endeavoured to lend a helping hand with counselling, acupuncture and herbal remedies like *Ginsavena* whenever I could.

One evening, I went with a group of people to a dark and miserable place in Antwerp (a large harbour town in Belgium), which was lit only by candles. I shall never forget the distressing scenes I witnessed there, too horrific to describe here. I realised then that it would be an uphill battle to tackle a problem of such magnitude. I concluded that addiction was one of the worst diseases that I had ever had to help with and I knew that I had to keep up the fight. Today, I am deeply saddened when I see how this particular problem has escalated. When I think of the medical advances during my lifetime and how this problem has increased, I am extremely concerned that I have not been able to do more. This is especially the case when I see useful young lives being destroyed when people are drawn against their will into this underworld, which often brings to an untimely end a life which could have been so worthwhile, if only more support and help had been available.

In the town in Holland where I was born, certain drugs are freely sold in inconspicuous backstreet shops. When I observe the unhealthy, dishevelled people going in and out of these establishments, I fear that the fight against this problem is beyond anyone's control, even though we are part of a society where each individual has the power to determine his own destiny.

One case which really shocked me was when I was asked to see a girl whose parents lived in Scotland and whom I had known for many years. Both parents were extremely hard working and held responsible positions. Their daughter had had a good upbringing and, at that time, was working in London. Unfortunately, she had become acquainted with a group of people who introduced her to drugs. As she did not realise their addictive powers, the drugs steadily took over her life. She had changed into a self-centred, aggressive, nasty girl. When I went to talk to her, she was quite open and cooperative, telling me all about her situation. She mentioned her disappointments in life and how these people had a listening ear. She had felt very lonely after going to London and, as a result, had become heavily involved in the practices to which she had now become addicted. During our conversation, I discovered that she was pregnant, which worried her greatly. She also told me that she desperately wanted to make something of her life and she felt that this baby was probably the answer. She did not know who the father of her unborn baby was and, basically, did not want to know. As my eldest daughter was a midwife in London at that time, I sought her advice on what the outcome would be for a young baby born of drug-using parents.

It was a lengthy process to help this girl but, using acupuncture and with help from others, we managed to wean her off the drugs. Luckily, by the time the baby was born, the young mother was in quite good health. Although the baby needed some treatment as she grew up, everything turned out all right. The love that she had, and which had been misused, was now focused on the baby.

It was fortunate that everything turned out well in that instance, after many struggles, fears and problems – but how many similar cases end in disaster?

I once took care of a young baby who was born of parents who were heavily dependent on drink and drugs. The authorities decided that the mother could not care for the baby and, fortunately, another family member was willing to shoulder this responsibility. This, coupled with the help I was able to give the baby, enabled us to bring this child into a society where, although her intelligence was slightly impaired, she nevertheless has grown into a lovely girl who is managing to face the world.

The fight against addictions continues. In addition to the battle with drugs, another major addiction to be tackled is alcoholism.

How many people in the world today are dependent on alcohol? For recovering alcoholics, it takes just one small drink for things to get out of hand. Over the years, I have treated some of the finest people who, because they have been unwilling to seek help for this enormous problem, have become outcasts from society.

I have often managed to help alcoholics regain a normal life, but when I look at the destruction resulting from alcohol, I realise how this problem is escalating and becoming ever more devastating.

I remember a gentleman of whom I was very fond and who had done a very great deal for society. He devoted his time, energy and even his own money to helping those less fortunate, especially disabled or abandoned children. Sadly, however, he slowly got into the grip of that incredibly addictive drug, alcohol. He lost sight of what was important and lost his possessions. Things went from bad to worse until, finally, it affected his health. His very supportive family and I did all that we could. Alas, nothing could prevent his untimely death from liver failure. As I stood at his grave, I recalled the many fights I had won during my life, yet this one I had lost. I had been unable to make his mind strong enough to overcome his disastrous alcohol addiction.

I have, however, often been victorious, helping people through such difficult times. If patients realise the damaging effects of alcohol on their health and agree to cooperate fully with any treatment I suggest, it is possible to overcome the problems and regain their quality of life.

A young woman who had been badly treated by her husband

came to see me. Very lonely and unable to sleep at night, she had started taking what she called 'a nightcap'. Alcohol, being so addictive, soon took hold. Unknown to some of her family, she became an alcoholic. Her health had deteriorated and she had become quite weak. I had many conversations with her, some quite lengthy. When I was finally able to reach her conscious mind, making her realise how this addiction was damaging her health and her life, and frightening her children, she started to cooperate with the help and treatment offered, and eventually overcame the addiction. I shall never forget her saying, 'I did not know what I was doing, but I know life has become very meaningful to me once more and my children recognise me again as their own mother.'

It is always unpredictable how quickly one can reach the mind. Sometimes one little sentence is enough to change an addict's thoughts into positively wanting to overcome their problems. I have always said, 'Where there is a will, there is a way.' If one really wants to overcome a problem with addiction, it can be done.

Over the years, I have seen many unhappy, unlucky people who turn to addictive substances which are not only capable of destroying their hopes and happiness, but also their lives. Alcohol is both a threat to our bodily health and one of the biggest factors in carnage on the roads.

The lowering of oxygen in the tissue cells is a great danger and, whatever the explanation, one has to realise that with the long-term use and overuse of alcohol, brain damage will result, following which one is often incapable of seeing things in a clear light.

During this 50-year fight to help those with alcohol dependency, I have seen poverty, sadness and unhappiness, but I still must battle on to help human suffering wherever I possibly can.

It is not only our character but also our mind that can be altered by the regular use of addictive substances. We realise this when we look at the countless people who were constantly warned of the serious effects of nicotine. Nicotine, often more addictive than alcohol, can be a real problem. When nicotine affects people's lungs or even their joints, I again use the phrase, 'It is not five minutes to twelve, it is five minutes past twelve,' to remind them that they must take action immediately. Yet we have seen the most intelligent people failing in their fight to overcome their addictions. However, I have helped countless nicotine addicts over the years through holding counselling sessions, usually in groups of 12, and giving them acupuncture coupled with remedies such as *Craving Essence*. Many patients have written to me saying how grateful they are that they managed to conquer this nasty, dirty habit.

A hospital pathologist once showed me the lungs of a recently deceased smoker. I shall never forget seeing the black deposits in the tissue and black shadows on the lungs in the X-rays. The waste material that had totally congested the lungs of this patient had, yet again, caused an untimely death.

Do smokers not realise what they are doing to their health as a result of their addiction to nicotine? Even a visit to a hospital ward where the harsh reality of smokers fighting for life is clearly visible is still not a strong enough sight to discourage them. The message has to become clear in the conscious mind in order to influence the subconscious mind in the decision to stop. For many, that is where the great difficulty lies. To get this point over, they have to look forward and visualise a better life, where they will have improved skin, better health, improved breathing and increased energy. There is so much to look forward to. As I write, I am looking at a postcard I received from a patient that says, 'I am now enjoying a wonderful holiday with all the money which I would have spent on cigarettes when I was on the road to committing suicide with that nasty addictive habit.'

A great deal of self-control is needed to overcome engrained habits, which is not easy. It is much less work simply to give in. Nevertheless, the achievement gained from attaining self-control is better than the challenge of winning a football match. To emerge victorious in a battle against oneself is much more rewarding and worthwhile.

Fighting addictions can be a very hard battle, and can often be lost. However, I was reminded again recently of the tremendous reward to be gained by overcoming these habits. A gentleman had been coming to me for a long time with incurable psoriasis. It completely covered his body and he failed to make any progress. His joints were showing all the signs of arthritis, and I told him that in these joints were nicotine deposits. That shocked him. He promised me that he would quit smoking, although I warned him that it would not be easy. In the end, he was successful. I was absolutely astonished when, within three months, his psoriasis had cleared up. I commented how worthwhile it had been for him to give up smoking, to which he replied that he now had the chance of a new and better quality of life. That made me so happy.

Some time later, a young woman sat beside me, puffing, panting and gasping for breath. She had struggled repeatedly to give up smoking, but had been unsuccessful on each occasion, so she had decided to give in. I told her that her health could be improved greatly if she stopped smoking, as its effects were very noticeable. Although I offered to help her, she was unwilling to try again. I feel powerless and full of regret in situations such as this, but I understand the feeling so well.

It came to my mind a few weeks ago when a lady offered me a piece of Lindt bitter chocolate – something that I love. Inwardly, I was asking myself, 'Will I, will I not?' Then I failed. I took a piece, which I love to have with a cup of tea. This is a very bad combination for a diabetic like myself. However, when I imagined the lovely taste of that piece of chocolate, I felt guilty. I knew that I would pay for it later, because I realised that I would probably start to perspire minutes after eating it and feel unwell. I then told myself to consider my patients, because I knew I would be unable to give them 100 per cent if I was battling with yet another setback in my diabetes and not feeling myself. Fortunately, such thoughts are usually enough to stop me surrendering to any temptation.

During the many years I have been in practice, I have seen numerous battles against many different forms of addiction. One very particular addiction comes to mind.

A young lawyer once consulted me. Although he had a beautiful wife, he was addicted to other women. When he discussed this problem with me, he said that every time he had been with another woman, he promised himself that he would never do it again. Being religious, he prayed for guidance, but each time he failed. He asked if I could offer an explanation. This is very difficult because human flesh is weak and weaknesses can take over. Sadly, his actions ultimately destroyed his marriage. He asked afterwards, 'Was it worth it? Why am I so weak? Why can I not overcome this battle?' I told him that he could only do so if he talked to himself and, with a lot of prayer and meditation, he could overcome the weaknesses of the flesh. He said he wished I could give him an example, so that he could accept, in his subconscious mind, what he was doing. I told him that the only examples are those people who have total self-control, which enables them to overcome the problem. I have met many people from different religious backgrounds who have achieved success by meditation, or joining a group to practise yoga, and thus have been able to overcome their addictions.

The great King David won victorious battles. He was a wonderful, spiritual man who appreciated God's tremendous love for him. Yet, although the Psalms show what a great man he was, he lost the battle against the weaknesses of the flesh. He battled with himself when he took the wife of one of his officers and even let that officer die in battle. The punishment was great and this awful deed followed him throughout the rest of his life.

Addictions can even be manipulated to people's advantage.

A famous London lawyer once pleaded with me to treat a young client of his who was addicted to gambling. He would even attack old ladies to get the necessary money to feed his habit. This lawyer said that if I could provide a statement that I would treat this man for his addiction, this could be sufficient to keep him out of prison. I told the lawyer that I would do no such thing, but that I would be prepared to treat his client and show him what he was doing wrong in order to bring him to his senses.

Addictions can be extremely strong and have to be recognised in order to treat them. The subconscious mind has to take on board the message from the conscious mind and realise that life can be damaged or even destroyed unless changes are made. It takes considerable effort and guidance to help deal with an addiction but the end results can be so worthwhile.

It is encouraging to see how we can succeed in overcoming addictions and our own human failings. This is not only the case with strong addictions such as drugs, nicotine and alcohol, but also with the addiction many children have to sugar. Mothers face a huge battle to discourage their children from eating cream cakes or sugar-laden chocolate bars that are so addictive. Sugar has brought many people to their knees, in particular because of the health problems associated with it. In my book *Realistic Weight Control*, I give many examples, especially of young, hyperactive or autistic children, who are addicted to certain ingredients within foods to which they might be allergic and yet which they crave. We see this with migraine sufferers when they crave chocolate while enduring a bad attack. The foods that cause the trouble are the very ingredients that one craves and eats during such times.

One encouraging point is that it only takes three weeks for the palate to become accustomed to the elimination of addictive substances. By withdrawing a specific item for three weeks, the palate no longer has any need for that particular substance. Consider people who take three or more spoonfuls of sugar in their tea or coffee. Withdraw the sweetener for two or three weeks and they will not like the taste of it when it is reintroduced. That is how we often have to look upon addictive problems. With children, we have to teach that it is not possible for them to have certain foodstuffs that are disastrous to their health. Psychological influence can help children overcome addictive tendencies while they are still very young. If, however, they continue along the path of addiction, it could result in disaster.

The worst offenders are refined carbohydrates (such as sugar and refined flour), food additives, chemicals and synthetic drugs, plus addictive and unsuitable drinks. Bad nutritional habits and an inadequate or uninspired diet, combined with other lifestyle factors, are very often the reason for addictive tendencies. I have regularly seen this when natural products are tampered with and turned into artificial products, which have nothing in common with the original. Products in their natural state help people stay healthy. The offending artificial foodstuffs are very often addictive. Some soft drinks even go so far as to contain addictive substances that encourage people to crave more of them.

A young girl who drank eight large bottles of a certain cola each day came to see me. Not only was she grossly overweight but, because of her addictive nature, her personality had totally changed. I pleaded with her to give up these drinks, although I knew it would not be an easy task. I finally had to give her acupuncture, after which she managed to stop. When her addiction ceased, I saw a changed girl. She had a different attitude and became much more active in her daily life.

A healthy body will metabolise natural sugars from fruit, raw vegetables and cereals, which contain all the original vital substances such as vitamins and minerals, without any problem. However, concentrated refined carbohydrates can cause a sudden sharp rise in the blood sugar level, which leads to an addictive condition that causes hypoglycaemia (a drop in blood sugar).

I realise that children like chocolate drinks. However, these drinks often contain 60 to 70 per cent sugar and, for this reason, they should be withdrawn from the diet. They also contain indigestible cocoa that contains caffeine and saturated fats. Once a child becomes addicted, this can trigger allergies, and the degree of saturation can be so high that when children eat or drink chocolate, they can lose their natural appetite. The biggest problem is that these drinks do not contain natural complementary substances that enable chocolate drinks to be properly digested. The same applies to plain chocolate, which is a vitamin and mineral robber.

We live in a world full of addiction. Nowadays, people prefer to drink coffee, black tea, milk chocolate drinks, soft drinks, cola, alcohol or milk (which is also quite indigestible), instead of healthy water. Coffee and other drinks containing caffeine stimulate the taste buds in the mouth; they also stimulate the digestive juices in the stomach, increase the heart rate and the functions of the brain, help temporarily against migraine headache and stimulate urine production and bowel movement. It is no exaggeration to say that some coffee drinkers drink eight or more cups of coffee per day. I see this regularly in the television and radio world, where broadcasters need these stimulants to keep them going. However, in the long term, coffee is a nerve poison. Cola drinks containing a lot of caffeine are often the cause of children being highly strung. Sleeplessness and depression are also some of the problems associated with such addictions. Similar reactions follow the consumption of alcoholic drinks, and those who make a habit of drinking alcohol may be creating severe health problems for themselves.

Since the First World War, the consumption of coffee and sweet drinks has increased tenfold and the number of alcoholics is now frightening. Because coffee and alcohol stimulate kidney function and water elimination from the reserves of the body, these types of drinks can truly dehydrate the body.

It is often realised too late that an addiction needs treatment and, by that time, it is a struggle to stop. This is why I often tell parents and grandparents not to feed their children with these addictive products.

When I look at the world today and at my practice, and see how people so easily mistreat their bodies over and over again, I am disappointed that more has not been done. It is not, as I often say, the quantity of life that is important, it is the quality of life that counts. When we look at the staggering figures of the increase in degenerative diseases, such as cancer, multiple sclerosis, diabetes, arthritis and so many others, I am convinced, after 50 years fighting for people's health, that poor dietary management and addictions to the wrong foods, drinks and inappropriate habits can be blamed for the horrific problems we are faced with today.

So the fight against addictions continues. Old habits can die, but then come quickly back to life again. The slightest mishap or stressful situation can lead addictive people to seek solace by returning to their old ways. Very often, without knowing, they are drawn back to that downward spiral, from where they were once so happy to have escaped.

I shall never forget a gentleman whom I greatly admired. His wife was one of my patients. He was a wonderful person and basically a loving husband, father and grandfather, but for many years he had been an alcoholic. He struggled against it most of his life until it almost killed him. His wife finally managed to persuade him to see me and we had a long chat. To cut a long story short, using acupuncture, counselling and herbal remedies I was able to help him and he stopped drinking. It was amazing to see how his liver regenerated. This is the only part of the anatomy that will regenerate if influenced positively. He gained a new lease of life.

Sadly, after many years, he sat before me again. I looked at him and I knew that he was in trouble. He said, 'Believe it or not, for seven years I have been in heaven. Now, I am back in hell.' He was back in the grip of his addiction and felt very lonely. He told me that his son had returned from Paris at

Christmas and brought a few bottles of liqueur. After dinner on Boxing Day, he poured out a glass of liqueur for everyone and, without thinking, he took a little glass himself. That same evening, he was back in the pub. He begged me to help him conquer this dreadful addiction once more and to help him understand that the minute he took another drink, he would be back on this downward spiral again. This is a lesson for all those I have treated and seen over the years. With an addiction, one has to put a stop to it very firmly, because the minute one develops an addiction – no matter to what – if a relapse occurs, one is fully back in its grip, which can result in disappointment and destruction.

CHAPTER FIVE

My Fight against Poison
and Pollution

After lecturing on this subject, I am often asked if we have reached the point of no return. I generally reply that we live by food, water and air. We have greater control of the first two if we take care of our diet but air is different. Here we need to become actively involved to improve matters, lobbying governments and environmental agencies, as I do, in the fight against air pollution.

We must all act now to protect the planet – this wonderful creation that God gave Man to enjoy. Time and again I have repeated Alfred Vogel's statement, 'In nature, everything is in harmony. What is out of harmony is Man's creation and we must do everything to make sure that what Man does is safe.'

While carrying out research for my book *Female Cancers*, I looked into the whole matter of poison and pollution, and concluded that it is not surprising that degenerative disease, for example cancer, has increased to the levels it has reached today.

While I was still working in pharmacy as far back as 40 years ago, at a time when penicillin and certain other antibiotics were freely available, and when farmers routinely came to collect ampoules of these drugs to inject into their cattle, I asked myself, 'How can this be good for Man?'

Years ago, I was quite intrigued to read an article on this topic written by Dr Benthem Oostrehuis, an elderly doctor from Amsterdam who, incidentally, lived to the remarkable age of 102. He claimed that antibiotics administered to animals were used too intensively and warned about their overuse. I travelled to Holland particularly to see this eccentric doctor and soon realised that we were both of the same opinion: it is not possible for these particular remedies to be freely used without harming people or animals. Together, we established an Association for Alternative Food and Drug Administration in Holland. A lot of people joined forces with us and we became very active. At one point I became suspicious about a particular factory and I urged the Dutch equivalent of the Milk Marketing Board to take a few samples of milk from its premises for analysis. When the tests showed the high percentage of antibiotics that were present in the milk and their possible poisonous influence, the Food and Drug Administration immediately ordered 650,000 pints of milk to be disposed of – and that was only one incident.

Consider the intensive use over many years of insecticides, pesticides and fertilisers to make grass grow more rapidly to feed cattle, together with all that Man has introduced (not only for himself but also for cattle). With these chemicals being slowly absorbed by the body through consumption of animal products it does not surprise me that such a monstrous disease as cancer is having its devastating effect on Man. I came to this conclusion many years ago when like-minded people and I discussed in depth how this would affect people's health.

I smiled to myself when I finally read in national newspapers that doctors were *now* warning against antibiotics being administered like sweets. Although I have nothing against antibiotics – Sir Alexander Fleming's realisation of the effect of penicillin on bacteria was indeed a great discovery – I am sure he would not have approved of people taking it so freely, or the extent to which it has gradually affected Man. For this reason, I have always said that caution must be exercised when using specific poisons or drugs as they could have a detrimental effect on health.

One lovely sunny morning, many years ago, a farming couple sat before me. I shall never forget them relating their symptoms to me. I listened carefully and found it incredible that the lady was describing an illness rarely heard of at that time, ME (myalgic encephalomyelitis). She was my very first ME patient. Her husband, on the other hand, showed all the symptoms of Parkinson's disease. The whole case puzzled me. They told me they lived in an area that was, by all accounts, a very healthy one. When I took a blood test from both patients my questions were answered as both revealed an accumulation of toxins in their systems. As the gentleman visibly showed characteristics of Parkinson's disease, I started to wonder about the whole situation. Quite a number of years later, I heard that many cows in that same area were dying of cancer. Following investigations, it was discovered that large amounts of artificial fertilisers were being used and that the farmers had been using pesticides such as Lindane for many years. As I mentioned in *Female Cancers*, Lindane is an organochlorine pesticide that has been extensively used in Western Europe for over 60 years. Serious health problems have been linked to this chemical. Human poisoning by Lindane has been reported throughout Europe and children are particularly susceptible to its toxic effects. It has also been noted as a possible carcinogen and an endocrine disrupter. The acceptable daily intake of its residues is very often exceeded. This pollutant is highly volatile and, when applied, the pesticide enters the atmosphere and is deposited by rain. Because it is fat soluble, it can appear in the food chain and leaves its residues in the kidneys, liver and tissues – not only in humans, but also in animals. It is for those reasons that I have been campaigning hard to get Lindane banned.

The case of that particular couple interested me so much that I rose from my bed in the middle of the night and went into my library. I had recalled reading that, in a few tests carried out in Australia, certain post-viral syndromes were detected and also that Parkinson's disease had been linked to the use of various pesticides, insecticides and fertilisers. It was reassuring to discover that what I had believed throughout the many years I have worked in this field was correct. It is astounding to realise how much poisonous and waste material is present in people's blood. Even with the younger generation, when I have the slightest inkling that a lymphatic problem may be present, I carry out tests to find out what is happening in the body. Nowadays, with the more modern equipment like the Vegacheck machine, we can get an indication of how much damage is being done to the system by one simple check.

We are natural beings, we live in nature, belong to nature, are part of nature and we need to keep life as natural as possible, because we have finally realised that, scientifically, things have gone too far. For many years I have campaigned against spraying crops and have appealed to countless farmers. In addition, Alfred Vogel and I have both written at length in magazines on the dangers of pesticide poisoning. The many articles published on poisons and pollution are always present to remind us of their dangers, and that we must take these matters seriously or pay the price for them.

It is the same with dental amalgam in teeth. One would think it impossible that every time we grind our teeth, a small particle of mercury enters our system, but if we think homoeopathically with its smallest potencies, we can then understand how things can easily go wrong. One can either have an allergy to the mercury, which can lead to bigger problems, or the blood is being constantly attacked.

There is nothing better for Man than clean blood. That is the reason I advocate detoxification and the continual cleansing of the system. It is quite surprising just how much better one feels following a detox programme. An excellent one that I recommend is Alfred Vogel's *Detox Box*. I can truly say that, having been in this field of medicine for half a century, it is crucial to keep our bodies as clean and pure as we possibly can.

My mind goes back to the time 50 years ago when I assisted in the pharmacy in Holland. I recollect people reporting how much better they felt when taking two or three garlic capsules at night. They had been taking various drugs, etc., but when they started to take simple garlic capsules – and you could say there is nothing more simple than garlic – they felt so much better. Why? Garlic is wonderful for cleansing the blood. It is an antiseptic, a deodoriser and, although it might have an unpleasant smell, it is of great benefit to health. I recall a time I was in the Swiss mountains with Alfred Vogel following heavy rain, when he fell onto his knees and started to dig in the heavy mud as soon as he smelled wild garlic. He pulled out a little garlic bulb and said, 'Look, even in all that mud and dirt its silvery-white colour shows us that God gave this to Man to keep his body cleansed.' Even outwardly, no mud had adhered to this small garlic bulb – a clear indication, as Vogel said, that it was to keep one's body clean.

I get exasperated when older people say that because things will not change during their lifetime, why should they concern themselves about the state of the planet, or that there is nothing they can do to change things anyway. Even though people sometimes criticise the younger generation, I admire those who do take action and are conscious that we have to protect this planet of which we are all a part.

I will never forget many years ago when Alfred Vogel and I gave a lecture in Australia on this subject. A group of young people approached us afterwards and asked if there was anything they could do to help. Because I had always been alarmed about the extensive use of the pesticide DDT, I suggested they could perhaps take some action against this chemical that was being widely used by farmers at that time. The harmful effects of DDT to Man, animals and the environment have been well catalogued. It is probably the one compound, above all others, that first sparked off concern about the possible adverse effects of chemicals on the environment. So they set up an action group and spearheaded a campaign to get the use of DDT prohibited.

Many years later, due to their hard work and commitment, the Australian Government banned DDT, and the restrictions throughout the rest of the world became much more stringent as a result of their efforts. This serves as a powerful reminder that any chemical introduced into the environment on such a large scale should initially be studied for any potential problems that may result.

It is very important that we consider ways to improve matters in order to protect our health. Sadly, we live in a world surrounded by drugs and materials that need to be cleared out. It is therefore essential that we keep active in our fight, looking not only at the harmful effects of poisons and pollution in the world today but also at the geopathic stress (from living under electric cables) that is all around us, in order to keep the energies in balance so that our bodies can function properly.

One patient asked me why people long ago believed in fasting. Fasting is a process of cleansing the system and giving the body a rest from its normal food intake, and, if undertaken sensibly, is beneficial to the functioning of the body. A blood sample taken from this lady revealed that a lot of waste material was present in her blood. She said she wanted to start on a fasting programme immediately, but I advised her against this course of action. Although I am keen on fasting, I recommended that we start by cleansing her system. I advised her to follow a sensible, healthy diet for a month and I prescribed a strong antioxidant and another brilliant remedy, now sadly no longer available to me. After a month, she returned and said she felt so well that she didn't really want to go ahead with the fast, but I advised her that then was the best time to do just that. I recommended that, if possible, she should aim to fast for a week by following a system I would devise for her, and then to come back and see me. She decided to do this for ten days, which would give her body a much-needed break. I understood exactly what she meant afterwards when she said, 'Now I feel clean.'

Isn't it a satisfying feeling when one cleans out a cupboard or a room and then, on inspection, is aware that it is a great deal tidier, a lot nicer and a much better environment? It is the same with the human body. It is a marvellous feeling when you are cleansed of everything that could possibly have damaged your system by healing the body's abnormalities. The problem could possibly have been constipation or even a constant cough or wheeze. There are so many ways you can cleanse your system and I have written at length in *Stomach and Bowel Disorders* and *Viruses, Allergies and the Immune System* on this subject. Over the years, I have dealt with many patients who have gone through the same treatment as that particular lady, resulting in their feeling really clean, healthy and able to cope with life's daily tasks.

It is all too easy to get into a rut, to take life for granted and plod along, not thinking of the consequences. Animals, which are almost invariably in greater contact with pollutions and poisons than humans as they are closer to nature, can suffer from their harmful effects, often more quickly than humans. Nowadays, we see so many people suffering from the mistakes made by previous generations. Certain poisons can trigger symptoms that can slowly lead to a dangerous situation and damage our body's cells. We need cell renewers, not cell breakers. We must therefore set aside time to take stock of what we are doing to our bodies.

I will never forget the dreadful consequences of the thalidomide drug. Pregnant mothers took it in good faith to prevent morning sickness. I remember the uproar in the pharmacy business in the 1960s when the terrible effects of this drug were made public – babies born with deformed or missing limbs. Even simple remedies that were used to treat travel sickness had to be taken off the market. Although many trials had been carried out on this drug, the body's reaction to it was devastating. It was interesting to read of the legal cases that followed its withdrawal from the market. I have often said that one cannot claim that a drug is not dangerous or has no side effects by merely undertaking a specific number of trials. We have to examine the long-term effects of such drugs.

I recall another drug that used to be prescribed for rheumatic conditions. When I realised patients were experiencing various problems while taking this drug, I started to question its safety. I voiced my fears to the Pharmaceutical Society and, after a few years, it was acknowledged that it had caused liver damage. I could list similar instances that I have witnessed during the many years I have been working in this field.

Nevertheless, it is not all doom and gloom. Nowadays, much more is being done to offer protection to patients and customers who are taking remedies or medicines. With prescribed drugs and, where permitted, with natural medicines, the possible side effects and contraindications are stated inside the packet. The controls on certain remedies are definitely much more stringent than ever before.

I only wish those same controls were applied to preservatives (in particular, the so-called 'E' numbers), pesticides and herbicides. Fortunately, when the directions for use are observed, then there will probably be no evidence of chemical damage. However, very often those instructions are not adhered to. All too often I see the consequences in the form of allergic reactions from the overuse of numerous substances.

I have great concerns about food allergies. If we look at the huge quantities of the additive monosodium glutamate, used simply to improve the flavour of particular foods, we can expect adverse consequences. Consuming foods containing such additives can cause headaches that are often ignored. Headaches should be seen as a friendly alarm bell to warn us that we must be wary of what we eat. A reaction to additives can result in an allergy or be a tell-tale sign that our body cannot tolerate such substances. These initial warning signals are often ignored. With prolonged use, the body becomes accustomed to the specific additive and, if one continues to eat a particular substance, it becomes poisonous to the body and can cause internal damage. This is often the case with babies. A baby, who cannot talk, will instinctively start to scream. This can be a warning sign that the baby's body cannot tolerate an ingredient in the food. Particular care has to be exercised with tinned baby foods to ensure that the baby can tolerate any additives.

There is a call for the increased consumption of organic foods. So often in lectures people have expressed the view that it is too expensive. However, if more people bought organic foods, then the prices would gradually fall to a more affordable level so that everyone could reap the benefit. The quality of food, animal welfare, environmental benefits and avoidance of GM ingredients are the main reasons why more and more people are turning to organic foods. However, the extra cost remains the biggest deterrent. I do realise that in order to feed the masses in a world with a rising population vast quantities of foods have to be produced quickly, but this is normally done without any consideration of the best or safest methods of cultivation. Unfortunately, the consumption of mass-produced foods leaves us asking ourselves, 'Is it safe?' The only way to reassure ourselves on that point is to consume, where possible, more organic produce, free of artificial pesticides, herbicides or fertilisers.

Because I have long been involved with organic farming, I have campaigned for safer pesticides. There are so many alternatives that can be used in order to control insects, and proper advice should be sought on the right way to go about it. It is unquestionable that those who eat mass-produced foods, which contain fewer vitamins, minerals and trace elements than good-quality organic foods, develop more deficiencies in their bodies. Organic farming calls for a lot of understanding, but if science would put more effort into its study, the true benefits would be more widely known.

We only have to taste organic foods to appreciate the difference. If we consider colonies of bees from countries where pesticides are forbidden, we only need to taste their honey to realise how delicious it is. During a lunch I shared with Alfred Vogel, he extolled the value of Guatemalan honey, its excellent taste and his pleasure in eating something that had not been tampered with and that he knew was safe.

There are numerous ways in which we can improve our food and help the environment. When I studied organic farming, I once asked one of my old gardeners if we could grow better leeks than those I had seen in Holland. I shall never forget his words. First he showed me a bed of strawberries, grown with the help of pesticides, herbicides and fertilisers, and asked me to taste one, which I did. He then showed me a similar bed, which he had grown naturally using compost that was completely safe and had been approved by The Soil Association. These strawberries were a bit smaller than the artificially grown ones and he again invited me to try one. Both the smell and the taste of the naturally grown strawberry were absolutely wonderful. He said that we could do the same with the leeks. With the use of natural compost, our leeks were even bigger than the ones I had seen in Holland and, more importantly, the taste was far superior. This natural cultivation had resulted in the leeks being much higher in minerals and having a strong immune system. I was delighted to be able to report on our tremendous results with those organically grown leeks, which are especially beneficial to diabetics, so that others could follow suit.

When I examine blood tests to try to establish where a problem lies, it is alarming to realise that it is not only the obvious chemicals like mercury amalgam that are harmful. Cooking salt already has a lot to answer for and is often used far more than is necessary, as is white sugar. These two culprits are often responsible for problems I have to help conquer nowadays such as high blood pressure, diabetes and obesity. It is a struggle to discourage people from consuming such products and I often have to stress the harm they can cause. Metallic salts are also extremely hazardous. Many are used in old-fashioned 'preserving' and food products, and they will eventually arrive in the lymph system, where they can cause a lot of damage.

Many patients have lymphatic congestion. I only need to look at the lymph glands in the neck, under the arms or between the legs for signs of this. The poisons or waste materials which have become lodged in those lymph glands have to be removed. I have covered this topic in *Questions and Answers on Family Health* and *Female Cancers* but, basically, the lymph glands, which during the night cleanse waste material gathered in the body over the course of the day, are often overworked. We have to ensure that we do not overload them. When there is toxicity in the blood or one feels unwell, the alarm bells of the lymphatic system start ringing.

When we scrutinise the contents in the wide array of aerosols used in and around the home – like hair lacquers, deodorants or insecticide sprays – it should be noted that many of the ingredients are poisons. One way or another, these substances will affect the bloodstream. It is not only the obvious things like chemical sprays that should concern us – the obscure ones can cause the most damage.

All these factors make us look at the numerous poisons surrounding us – the pollution and poisons in the air or the pollution in the water caused, for instance, by the dumping of everything from old computers to dangerous waste, which not only affect us in the Western world, but people everywhere. If we look at pots and pans made from aluminium, it is easy to understand how this metal can get into our systems through the cooking process; or consider the synthetic fibres we wear, with which we are in constant contact, or the plastic containers in such regular use, while some materials even contain considerable electromagnetic energy. Body energies have to cope with a lot. If they are positive, they will be to our benefit. However, if these are negative, problems can arise. I have seen many patients over the years who, to put it simply, are victims of an environment created by Man. I have dedicated time and effort through my books and elsewhere to warning against pollution and asking for help in the ongoing fight.

When working in some underdeveloped countries, I have witnessed the results of ruthless management in the use of harmful or dangerous products and materials. Some time ago I visited Ghana and Sri Lanka, where I met with representatives from the Ministry of Health and had the opportunity to look around. Not only was I alarmed by the climatic influences in these countries, but also by the circumstances in which the people lived. In Zambia, I was shocked to see all the hospitals crammed with AIDS patients, as well as those crippled with rheumatic diseases. The latter may be caused by their hot and humid climate, or their unhealthy diet.

Yet I have visited countries where degenerative diseases are fairly rare. I once visited South-west Africa, where the people endure a constantly hot, sauna-like climate, yet there were virtually no rheumatic diseases. We learned there how *Devil's Claw*, which they were taking almost on a daily basis, was a great help not only in keeping their kidneys cleansed, but also providing the natural salts necessary for their daily diet. It is important to keep the balance right in order to maintain a healthy system. If one aspect is out of balance, the others become imbalanced, yet it takes so little to return the situation to normal. Therefore, with a little effort and guidance, one can reach one's goal of better health.

We can see the first signs of the greenhouse effect today – the summer of 2003 gave us an indication of what can happen. The effects of the sun's very hot rays were very noticeable. In a greenhouse, plants will soon wither and die from the effects of excessive sunlight if they are not watered at the right time or do not receive the correct amount of moisture. It is the same for human beings, as overexposure to the sun's rays can result in sunburn and skin cancers. Again, balance is essential or problems will arise.

One of the most difficult journeys I have ever had to make was to a cemetery where a young mother was buried. A few months earlier she had given birth to her third baby. She had become an innocent victim of today's society as, unknown to her, chemical poisoning entered her system and destroyed her nerve tissue before finally taking a beautiful young life that filled such a worthwhile place in society. This is what worries me today – that Man, who was entrusted with Mother Earth, is gradually destroying the beautiful creation in which we live, but I cling to the great hope that all will become new again.

CHAPTER SIX

My Fight for Complementary Medicine Education

My primary school education was very disrupted, as the majority of it took place during the Second World War. Although nursery school went smoothly, difficulties arose during my primary school education, as there were frequently neither heating nor teaching premises available because of the conflict. Primary school started well and I had a wonderful teacher who sometimes came to school in a horse-drawn carriage. As an enticement for me to be obedient – I was quite a naughty child – she would pledge to take me home in her carriage, as she lived near my house. That was very exciting. So, all was fine during that initial period and I started to love school.

When our school was taken over by the Germans to be used as a pigsty, our schooling became very sporadi, as we were moved from pillar to post – an occasional day here and there in a church or in a hall. At that time, things were more geared towards fun than learning. Eventually premises were found where we could be given a more stable education. However, this was short-lived, as it emerged that the teacher was a collaborator and had been using the children as a means of gathering information for the Germans.

It was not until primary 5, therefore, that I realised how hard I would have to work to catch up. I was lucky enough to receive a lot of encouragement from my teacher in primary 6 – Mr Nyboer – and we became good friends. One of the photographs in this book shows that particular class. I greatly admired him and he had an immense influence on my life. Although he had been informed of my disruptive and rebellious behaviour at school, he had a knowledge of child psychology that was the best I had ever come across, and knew how best to help me. On days when there was no schooling available, he often gave me private tuition to help improve my levels at school.

The headmaster – who disliked me – told him not to waste his time and was very rough with me. To make matters worse, I got little support from my mother, who always sided with the teachers. Once, when I had been naughty again, the headmaster lost his temper, threw me out of the classroom and beat me to such an extent that my mother returned with me to the school for an explanation of what had happened. The headmaster apologised profusely, admitted to my mother he had gone too far, but explained how I had disrupted the whole class yet again. My mother, in his presence, gave me another slap around the ears and said she would make sure I would never do that again.

By the time I started further education, I realised that if I was to make something of my life I would have to work hard. I actually became quite a hard-working student, which certainly made up for the lack of interest I had shown at primary school. I quite enjoyed further education after acquiring this thirst for knowledge. I even attended a wide range of courses until I was well into my 50s to achieve a better understanding of what education really meant.

It was after meeting the Swiss naturopath Alfred Vogel in 1959 that I decided to dedicate my energies to complementary medicine. I was fascinated by all he had to say, finding the principles of alternative medicine most interesting. Regrettably, there were then only a limited number of institutions in Holland where one could gain knowledge and understanding in this field of medicine. The Germans, on the other hand, were quite familiar with alternative medicine – sometimes called natural medicine. They had become more aware of homoeopathy and naturopathy under the reign of Hitler, and '*Naturpraktiker*' was thriving there before the War because both Hitler and Himmler were extremely knowledgeable in this field. Countries such as Germany and Switzerland led the way and the theories of Carl Bilz, Sebastian Kneipp and many others were widely accepted. When the Germans invaded Holland, the Dutch homoeopaths and the handful of naturopaths were extremely keen on the Hitler regime simply because they finally received the help they had always wanted. To show their gratitude for this help, many sadly joined the NSP (the National Socialist Party). For that reason, when the War ended, anyone in Holland who was remotely connected to this field of medicine was virtually ignored and labelled a betrayer of their country. Therefore, when I started working alongside Alfred Vogel, it was very difficult to educate the Dutch people in the principles of natural medicine because its very name had been brought into such disrepute. That is why, in 1961, when the Inspector of Health became aware of what Vogel, my Dutch colleagues and I were doing, he called for me to be imprisoned and threatened to strip me of my orthodox certificates.

There was very little we could do until well into the 1960s when the understanding of alternative medicine became more recognised and young people's desire to study this branch of medicine became greater. When I bring to mind the changes that have since taken place and the hard work of pioneers to gain recognition, it is gratifying to see them now reaping the fruits of their labours.

Most doctors in Holland have some knowledge of natural medicine and most have undertaken courses in different disciplines to enable them to offer multi-disciplinary practices to their patients. Throughout Holland, education in alternative medicine is now much more advanced than in most other parts of the world.

When I arrived in Scotland in 1970, I realised that people's knowledge still had a long way to go and that was why I wanted to promote alternative medicine there. Realising how little was available in Britain, I knew a lot of work lay ahead of me if I was to succeed in integrating orthodox medicine with alternative medicine to create a system of complementary medicine. In order to do this, however, I had to study further to gain British qualifications. When I look back over the years since I came to Scotland, fighting for the recognition of homoeopathic and naturopathic treatments, it is gratifying that people have gradually become more aware of the immense benefits these healing methods can achieve.

I recall an evening in 1971 in the Turf Hotel in Ayrshire where my wife and her friends from boarding school days met for reunions. The well-known Scots actor Rikki Fulton – our wives had been friends since those schooldays – said, 'If you want to get anywhere with alternative medicine in Scotland, it will need a lot of education to show the benefits that it can bring.' The Turf Hotel's owner, a relation of Sir Alexander Fleming and known to all as Aunt Nettie, agreed, saying that I would need both to educate people and to have scientific proof that it really worked. Although I had just arrived in the country, I knew they were right. From that day, I have done everything possible to bring greater awareness of this field of medicine to Britain. There have been many mis-understandings surrounding alternative medicine, but we are steadily getting there. The immense thirst for further knowledge of complementary medicine, coupled with its growth and development, is proof of this.

In order to work towards my goal, I began giving lectures in hospitals. Back in the 1970s, it was difficult to convince medical students of the benefits of using alternative medicine and I faced many fights with critics, but I was lucky enough to lecture to postgraduates at the University of Edinburgh Medical School. As hardly any time was devoted to this field of study in universities at that time, they knew nothing about the topic and were often incredibly grateful for the lectures. Some of those students even went on to specialise in this field of medicine. It gives me such pleasure when I see throughout England, Scotland, Ireland and Wales that some of those same students have flourishing practices today.

So, that was the beginning.

I consulted for many years at 10 Harley Street in London, with around 60 other orthodox and alternative practitioners. At our meetings, we often discussed the call for further education, and the recognition that documentary proof was needed to support our claims. Of course, that was exceedingly difficult, because while governments would grant funding to further research in orthodox medicine, similar financial assistance was not offered to alternative medicine. So, whilst the orthodox practitioners had sufficient money to prove themselves, the alternative practitioners had to do it themselves. Often the only proof that alternative medicine worked at that time was the sight of waiting rooms full of patients seeking help. The practitioners could then demonstrate its efficacy by saying, 'Here you are. These patients are better and one cannot argue with results.'

I continue to travel throughout the world educating people in the principles of alternative medicine. In America and Canada, I was able to help establish an appropriate teaching programme, lecturing in many of their universities and alternative medicine colleges (which have now become universities). It gives me great pleasure to witness this expansion, to the extent that I even joined several committees at some of these universities.

Whenever I took part in radio programmes on CHML in Hamilton, Canada, I would take the opportunity of lecturing at the neighbouring McMaster University to give students an understanding of my work. It was the same in America. The need to educate people was enormous and a lot of work had to be done to get the message across to as many people as possible.

Back in Britain, in the late 1970s and early 1980s, alternative practitioners were gradually starting to establish themselves. The BCNO (British College for Naturopathy and Osteopathy), which is possibly the most advanced in both disciplines, was steadily becoming recognised as one of the top colleges in Britain. The same applied to the field of acupuncture and other alternative therapies. At long last, some universities had wakened up to the fact that there was a need for further education and recognition in this field of medicine and they then started to introduce the first forms of alternative medicine, nutrition and many other therapies to their programmes.

There was a great need to make alternative treatments more freely available to patients. However, many people were sceptical and wanted to know how they could be sure if the practitioners were recognised in their field and had received a proper education in alternative medicine or if they were quacks. Those questions were asked many times when I broadcast with Gloria Hunniford on her radio programme, as far back as the 1980s. I discussed the issue with many people in the public eye, whom I had treated as patients, and I often asked them for their support in spreading the word – people like Cliff Richard, Donny Osmond and many other famous singers, sports people and supportive journalists. Still, it was a fight, but a fight that was, little by little, marching uphill to victory. Although we are not quite there yet, we are nearing our goal.

I remember one occasion when, feeling quite distressed about further misunderstandings from the orthodox world, I received a call to visit a well-respected oncologist in this country. When I arrived at his beautiful home, this gentleman pleaded for help because he had almost come to the end of the road in his own life. We talked at length and it became apparent that he was extremely interested in alternative medicine and was open-minded enough to encourage me to persevere in what I was doing and to find more ways of educating universities with a view to increasing their understanding of this field of medicine. Even our well-loved Queen Elizabeth offered me advice on how to tackle the difficulties I was facing and, in fact, many members of the Royal Family have encouraged me to soldier on. I am happy to say that although the battle has not been won – especially nowadays against the drug industry – we are still gaining ground. As I have said in an earlier chapter, honesty will always win.

There are some professors who are bursting with knowledge and scientific facts, but if they lack understanding or the human ability to recognise the needs of those patients who have come to the end of the road with regard to orthodox treatments, then they are of little help in the fight to alleviate human suffering. On the other hand, we have the simple, sometimes less well-educated practitioners who, through their hands-on work, can relieve the pain and suffering of so many. Throughout the world, I have seen uneducated people who possess this special gift – probably handed down from grandparents and parents – who through working with their hands, and with simple, safe treatments, are able to help so many people in need.

I have given hundreds of seminars to practitioners, throughout the country, to encourage them to study and educate themselves and gain recognition in their field. They need to become aware of the basics of how to deal with people and, in order to ensure the safety of the public, they must be totally aware of what they are doing. Many have gone down different paths in their field of study, whether it be massage, reflexology, homoeopathy, aromatherapy, or perhaps the most important one that I have taught them – sympathy and compassion for the patients seeking help. That need is massive and requires to be met.

A number of years ago, I was asked by Queen's University, Belfast, to undertake postgraduate training seminars in the Pharmaceutical Department. These were designed to provide basic information on the products that the public were seeking and on the disciplines used in complementary medicine. What I found unbelievable was that the Government instructed a locum to be present to evaluate my seminars. I felt it an immense accomplishment when looking

91

at the evaluations after each seminar to note that I had scored very high levels of acceptance on each occasion, once almost 90 per cent. I believe the interest engendered by these seminars has been beneficial on many fronts. For example, one particular pharmacist increased turnover sixfold after becoming aware of what people wanted and recognising which remedies had proved to be particularly beneficial.

I decided to write *The Pharmacy Guide to Herbal Remedies* to assist them. Of all the many books that I have written on the subject of complementary medicine, that one is used almost daily in countless health stores and pharmacies as a quick and easy reference guide to the remedies people can take safely and those which have to be taken more cautiously.

Alfred Vogel and I organised several educative courses, as have others. The UK arm of Bioforce, under the direction of my daughter Janyn and her husband Dr Jen Tan, established an invaluable distance-learning course on Phytotherapy (plant medicine), which continues to be of immense help to doctors, pharmacists and practitioners who all have a responsibility to care for people's well-being. This course is probably one of the most valued courses in the industry and is one that I have personally endorsed many times.

I always gain great pleasure when I hold lectures throughout the world to see the enormous need and thirst there is for more information. We know that knowledge and education are vital to establish a recognised system. People here in Britain have fought so hard for this understanding – not just in my time but even as far back as 100 years ago. They have done all they possibly could to bring this knowledge into the field of education. A few I have admired immensely are Sidney Rose-Neil, Joe Goodman, Keith Lamont, Walter Thomson . . . but there are so many others who have also done their best to share their vast knowledge with those who are eager to learn.

Whenever I meet my friend Roger Newman Turner, who has also done everything he can for complementary medicine education, we talk with admiration of those who have left the legacy of tirelessly working towards the goal of a multi-disciplinary system to ensure that human suffering can benefit from the diverse methods that have been practised over hundreds of years.

I was extremely encouraged when the principal of Queen Margaret University College in Edinburgh personally asked me to assist in developing the education of students of complementary medicine, a task already begun by Professor Anne de Looy and her staff. I have donated to them my large collection of books, inherited from Alfred Vogel, Dr Len Allan and many others who studied these subjects in great depth, which will find a home in their new Craighall campus in East Lothian.

When I look at the research work undertaken by the well-known practitioner Dr Allan, which he outlines in his books, I now realise what an extraordinary researcher he was. Establishing an extensive library, covering every aspect of alternative medicine, is of enormous assistance to students, who can only benefit from this man and others having put their wide-ranging knowledge and understanding down on paper.

Probably one of my proudest moments was when I was granted the Professorship in Complementary Medicine at Queen Margaret's – the first such chair in Scotland – in recognition of my work in the field of naturopathic medicine and the development and promotion of the wider field of complementary medicine to the general public.

It gives me the greatest pleasure when I think of the medical people who, having spoken with me or attended my seminars, have introduced some of these multi-disciplinary therapies into their orthodox practices. It is pleasing not only to see how busy and how outstanding they are but, above all, to know that the patients get the help they deserve to alleviate their suffering. Many of these patients have come to the end of the orthodox road and, as a last resort, they turn to alternative therapies, the benefits of which are often beyond human understanding.

It is an uphill battle to establish education in complementary medicine. At long last, after 50 years fighting, the goal is in view and there is a warm feeling in our hearts because, over the years, we have proved it really works.

CHAPTER SEVEN

My Fight for Understanding

Many times during my life I have been aware of the true meaning of the word 'understanding'. I have possibly learnt this the hard way, but, in so doing, it has enabled me to display a great deal of understanding when it is needed – although, when I have not met with the understanding I seek in return, I experience a sense of failure. One needs to be willing to cooperate with what is being offered and one must be prepared to show this same understanding in return.

Understanding is essential in the world in which we live. We are all conscious that the nation is becoming increasingly selfish – a matter of 'I'm all right Jack'. We live in a world where we must offer support to each other and not act as though we are some of the first people to live on this Earth. When Cain murdered his brother, Abel, and God asked him where his brother was, Cain replied, 'Am I my brother's keeper?' Yes, we are. We have to help each other, but we must also have understanding from both sides, accepting the reality of life and recognising what we can and cannot do.

Whilst writing on this subject, I am reminded of the time when, a number of years ago, I was president of the British and European Osteopathic Association. We had quite a lot of members and, at one of our meetings, one member lodged a complaint concerning the actions of another, accusing him of trying to drum up extra business by handing out leaflets in which he made claims about the treatment he was providing and attempting to poach patients from the area in which this practitioner worked. As we were extremely strict on such matters and members had to abide by our rules and regulations, two written warnings were sent to him, without success. After a third and final warning, he was asked to attend a meeting. A number of those present asked why he could not build up his business by other methods, or if he was having financial problems. He said he had no financial worries, nor could he see any problem in handing out these leaflets.

I had to tell him in no uncertain terms that we had no alternative but to expel him from the Association. When he realised that he had gone too far and that I meant what I had said, he had tears in his eyes. He eventually admitted that he needed the patients. I tried to understand his problems. It was a Sunday and from the pavement under the window of the hotel room in which we were meeting I heard the

At school, looking after the invalids. I am in the front row, first left, standing.

Just engaged!

At the age of 18.

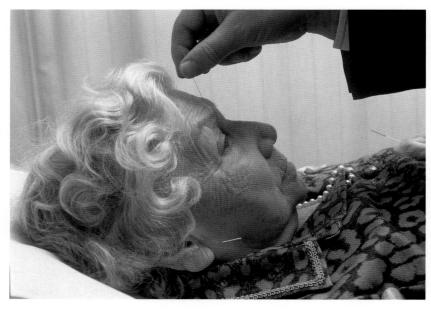

In action with acupuncture.

Performing iridology in New York.

Always educating other practitioners.

Leading a tour of the herbal gardens
at the Melbourne Botanic Gardens.

With the president of the
Australian Herbal Society.

In the Botanic Gardens in Glasgow launching the Jan de Vries
Benevolent Trust with patron Hayley Mills, second from right.

On a vegetarian cooking demonstration
television programme in Portland, Oregon.

In Canada, giving more information after a lecture.

Looking after horses!

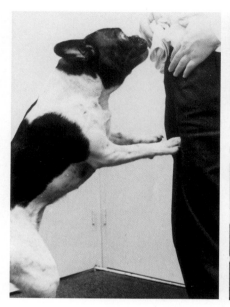 

This is Bobo, our second
French bulldog.

Tamara, our Samoyed, whose
story is in this book.

Tamara with her son, Raja. The smaller of the two is Tamara.

Opening yet
another clinic.

In my role as president of the British and European Osteopathic Association.

With Gloria, fighting for recognition of complementary medicine.

With some of my faithful supporters.

Salvation Army band playing 'Jesus Died for Sinners'. I smiled inwardly and asked myself how we could be so hard as to take away this man's bread and butter. So, for a third time, we forgave him, on the strict condition that he would never repeat his tactics.

This is all part of life. It is wonderful to experience forgiveness, but if one repeats the same mistake over and over again, forgiveness will not be so forthcoming, and understanding will go out of the window. It is very important though to try to understand both sides of a situation.

It is wonderful to receive credit for one's work. Not only is it of great encouragement to have approval from reputable associations but it also offers the public peace of mind when deciding which practitioner to consult.

I experienced tremendous love and understanding from the Northern Institute of Massage and Manipulative Therapies. Not only are their study courses very well grounded but the sole aim of members is to help alleviate human suffering. At every meeting that was arranged – and I would like to give a special thanks to Ken and Audrey Woodward, who organised these – the welfare of the public was their top priority, then the practitioner, then networking. The Society has stood the test of time for well over 80 years and maintains these fundamental principles. Our annual meetings were most enjoyable and I was often overwhelmed by the tremendous sense of love and understanding within the Society and the enthusiasm to educate and protect the well-being of the public. It was therefore a great honour for me to be invited to become their president in 1991–2 and I was also privileged later to be made a Fellow of that very worthwhile Society. When I think of all the good work that they have done and of the guidance they have given to many leading osteopaths in their chosen careers, I am thankful that I was once president of that Society. It is with immense pleasure that today I can see the fruits of all their hard work.

The British Naturopathic and Osteopathic Association, founded by eminent people like Stanley Lief, John Thomson and many others, operated for many years before merging with the Osteopathic Association of Great Britain in 1991. They worked tirelessly to establish an organisation encompassing naturopathy and osteopathy in Britain. It is with great pride that today we still have the British Naturopathic Association, which basically follows the principles of the great forefathers in this field. When I see people like Roger Newman Turner and Joe Goodman striving to maintain the high standards of medical care in our profession, then I am extremely proud to be associated with those colleagues who, selflessly, do their best to alleviate human suffering.

A lot of these old-fashioned therapies have been tried and tested. We see this with the well-established British Acupuncture Association, of which I have been a member for many years, where they have worked diligently on educative matters and have succeeded in promoting public safety. There are too many to mention here, but when I think of people like Sidney Rose-Neil, Jack Worsley, Mary

Austin, Eric Welton Johnson, Victor Foster, Keith Lamont and many more who have put every effort into fighting for their Association and its beliefs with the aim of establishing acupuncture as a much more acceptable and readily available part of medical treatment today, I am privileged to have been associated with them.

It has been with great conviction that those people, including myself, have fought for the acceptance and understanding of our disciplines that now benefit from the vast amount of research and work carried out over the years. I have taken part in hundreds of television and radio broadcasts with the sole objective of getting our message across to as many of the public as possible.

It is so distressing to see money, selfish attitudes and misunderstandings being constantly responsible for a great number of rifts that could easily be avoided if everyone joined forces and worked together for a more understanding society. Sadly, jealousy can also play a major role in destroying what could otherwise have been so good.

This same problem is apparent in the drug industry, where the primary consideration appears to be profit. Regretfully, many companies, instead of ploughing back their profits to improve the quality of products, seem to have been reaping the benefits at the expense of the public, and are trying to destroy what was once good. When I look at how ruthlessly those powerful industries go about their work, doing so little to further the research into what God has created for Man in his promise to give him the foods for his existence and the herbs for healing, my heart is deeply saddened. Their selfish attitudes are focused purely on economic growth and profits at any cost – even human lives – in a society where understanding and compassion is far from their minds.

Unfortunately, this problem exists in every country where people put profit before the well-being of others. I have sometimes watched with tears in my eyes as health inspectors have cleared the shelves of the natural products God gave Man to help himself. It is heartbreaking to see such powers destroying what was slowly building up to be such a great help to humanity.

I am so appreciative when I meet people who put their heart and soul into helping others and show understanding and compassion to their fellow human beings. The extent to which they are prepared to go to achieve this is often beyond human understanding. Once or twice in my lifetime, I have come across this wonderful experience.

Many years ago, when I was struggling to win for alternative medicine the recognition it deserved, I phoned practitioner and writer Michael van Straten to ask for help. When I told him about my problems, he offered support and sound advice, including a recommendation that I join the British Naturopathic and Osteopathic Association, which I mentioned earlier in this chapter.

It is comforting to know that there are some people we can turn to in life who have the ability to understand problems and are willing to help. I have always made an effort to correct myself when I have been too impatient about something, and cannot be faulted for striving to understand people's needs. I have always done my best to understand the great needs of this huge selfish world in which we live, where we ought to be each other's keeper.

Over the years, people have often asked, 'How can I learn understanding?' This is something we actually develop through time and it may be necessary to experience many difficult situations in life before we can truly show empathy towards others.

In the first part of this chapter, I consciously chose to relate the story of the osteopath who completely understood what we meant when he was told he could not continue as he was doing. The problem was that, because of his situation, and possibly greed, he initially made the decision to ignore the understanding behind our message. It is often difficult to accept and understand the message because it is not always what we want to hear.

I was aware of this on a visit to one of London's leading hospitals. The discussion focused on a certain product – *IP-6* and *inositol* – and its use as an extra boost in the treatment given to cancer patients. One doctor was totally open-minded and listened, trying to understand the message of Professor Shamsuddin who, having been in medicine himself for 30 years, researched this product and suddenly realised he had found what appeared to be a way of controlling cancer cells. This doctor understood that message, and was grateful for the little I could tell him about it and the literature I gave him on the product. On the other hand, his colleague was very negative. He didn't want to understand the message, because he was so locked into his own thoughts and the views cemented in his mind by his teachers so, without further investigation, he declared that there was nothing in it and it would be useless. He was not prepared to open his mind to this understanding.

Over the 50 years I have been in alternative – now more commonly called complementary – medicine, I have become so frustrated when I witness this narrow-minded attitude. When lecturing at universities both in Britain and abroad, I have often simply asked the questions, 'Do you know what I am talking about?', 'Do you understand the message in what I am saying?' I sometimes have to be quite blunt and almost rude in order to give students an understanding of something that they are either unwilling to come to grips with or to study. The Queen herself once said to me that it was necessary to have an open mind on everything and to make certain that no opinionated or predetermined frame of mind dismissed something from which we could learn so much. Would it not make more sense to give a particular remedy a chance, even to study it or perhaps try it, especially when there is evidence that it does work?

One cannot always provide total understanding. Here is a simple example. For many years I have taken part in radio and television programmes, and I have never felt embarrassed in recommending to those with painful knee joints that they place a fresh cabbage leaf over the knee, leave it there overnight and feel how much better the knee is the following morning. A long time ago, I was treating a hospital matron in the same way. I met her GP in a corridor and he looked at me and said, 'Jan, you are an intelligent man, so how can you possibly think that putting cabbage leaves on the matron's knees will cure her problem?' I told him it wasn't a cure, but a help. Immediately – as anyone else would probably do – he asked, 'But how does it work?' One explanation is that there is acidity in a cabbage leaf that draws out any inflammation, but there are all kinds of possible reasons. Simply put, one cannot argue with results. If something works, then I say that it does not matter how it works, as long as it is of help. Over the years, I have witnessed so many things that are beyond human understanding.

CHAPTER EIGHT

My Fight for Peace and Love

Those two little words – 'peace' and 'love' – are inseparable. Where there is love, there is generally peace, and vice versa. These emotional issues are very close to my heart and I feel that we all have the ability within us to achieve peace and to love others as we really should.

My struggle with the word 'peace' goes back more than 50 years, to a time when I was growing up amid the Second World War and peace seemed very distant. I witnessed the fighting that had escalated between the nations, the arguments that took place in people's homes and the tensions that broke out in the streets when starving townsfolk literally fought over a piece of bread. Hostility between people was all around us and, even at my young age, the seeds of hate were being sown against the enemy. This was something that was bred into us during the War and if we, as children, had the opportunity to play a dirty trick on the German occupiers we would do it, because we all wanted to play some small part in hampering the enemy's encroachment on our homes and country.

It was inevitable that the hatred being implanted in those young hearts would have repercussions in later life. I still see the hateful ramifications of that 'bloody war' today in my home country of Holland. We should have learned that if we all loved our neighbour as ourselves, then that war could have been avoided.

When the Second World War ended, I saw the happiness on the faces of people who had been given back the freedom to live a normal life. Everybody expressed their wish for a peaceful existence and felt that now was the time to unite behind one religion and one political party, and to join forces to build a better country where peace would reign. People were so thankful when the War ended that there was harmony and togetherness. Those thoughts now seem so far away, as Holland has never been so divided, with its large blend of religions and more political parties than any other country in the world.

I have had the privilege of travelling to 61 countries and have lectured in 40 states of America. During my travels, I have looked around at what could be achieved by peace. I have often asked myself, 'What is peace?' and 'What sacrifices can we make to ensure peace throughout the world?' The great desire I have deep in my heart to be an instrument of peace is sometimes rudely disturbed when I see how seemingly minor incidents can easily trigger disharmony. By learning to understand ourselves better and by exercising the powers we have within us to exhibit peace and love, we will not only heal ourselves but we will also have the capacity to make a difference to the world – a world that is often deeply divided and miserable.

Making a difference does not need to cost money – we only have to understand a few points on how to show gratitude to our Creator. I often recount a short passage from the Old Testament when thinking of what our contribution should be to creation and to our Creator. When it was asked, What could we do?, the response came that it was not measured by great gifts, or in rivers of oil, or even sacrificing our firstborn – there are only three things necessary: first of all, to act justly; second, to show our merciful love and third, to walk humbly with our Creator (Micah 6:7–8).

On the surface, these three requirements seem fairly straightforward. However, if we think about it methodically, it will probably take a lot of effort, but to strive for peace and love would be a great achievement. We perhaps only ponder these matters, but how good it is to know that when we put these thoughts into action, we will succeed, and we will then become an instrument of peace and love in this heartless world.

I often ask myself what the word 'peace' really means. Throughout the world, I have talked to many patients who probably became ill because they were powerless to create peace or unable to show or to accept love. To become a being or a spirit of love means healing. Every true and sincere desire to exercise healing is extremely important.

Love is the greatest force in the universe. It is the principle of all life and the basis of all existence. To love in the true sense of the word is to heal, and to love greatly is to possess immense healing powers. The soul of love is the pure and strong desire to bless, to share and to impart all our goods to others, and we need to have the capacity to show love unconditionally. Our ability to express love will grow through experience, and when we care for everybody with the same measure of love that we demand for ourselves, our power to heal will then become a natural emotion and unfailing every time.

Peace, however, is an atmosphere of the main essentials in our life. If we move into absolute silence and instil calm depths in our mind, then higher powers are found, as consciousness cannot enter into the deeper states of real life. The true being cannot be fully realised until a peaceful state is thoroughly established in mind and body. Silence is the great signature of peace, and the reality and understanding of silence will enhance our understanding of what peace is all about.

I became more aware of this during the revolution in Sri Lanka, when I was asked to help treat some of the refugees in one of the hospitals there. The hatred that spurred on the fighting between the Tamils and the Singhalese was so intense that they were bloodthirsty for each other's wives. But when they returned injured from battle and required hospital treatment, I witnessed some of those very hard hearts melting as they experienced love and care. It is of great help when the spirit is reminded of how wonderful love can be. In moments of tranquillity, I spoke to some of those ruthless fighters, when a sense of inner peace had eventually reached their souls. One can make a start in achieving peace by ensuring a tranquil environment during medical treatment, knowing that the deeper the peace, the more potent the healing force stimulated and, consequently, the greater the results.

This was very visible during the years I worked in Northern Ireland, where the hatred between opposing groups within its society caused hostility for almost 30 years and innocent blood to flow. Whether it was for religious or political reasons, the hatred was so fierce that the struggles they endured were visible. But wasn't it incredible that some of the parents of the innocents killed showed a spirit of forgiveness and love for their fellow beings, so that some of those intolerable conditions could be turned around? Astonishing transformations took place when some of those who were badly affected by this ruthless, senseless war became more forgiving and made a conscious effort to accept an almost unforgivable situation. By learning to acknowledge their circumstances, they forgave their enemies and, in so doing, created an atmosphere encompassing forgiveness, peace and love.

We see this in hospitals, nursing homes, hospices and other places where sick and afflicted people are nursed and cared for. Those peaceful and tranquil surroundings, combined with care, will help the weary sufferers more than any medicines. These experiences are often great healers.

I once worked in a hospital where there was an elderly nurse. When patients argued with each other, or with the nurses, she would refer to a biblical expression that anger was 'the rotting of bones'. In her wisdom, she told them that their conditions would worsen if they didn't change their attitude. I have often witnessed occasions where hatred, jealousy or unnecessary quarrels have caused people's conditions to deteriorate.

I have pleaded repeatedly with many patients to try to find a harmonious solution to some of their troubles, and have explained how important it is to overcome their problems, no matter the cause, because anger, jealousy and hatred will always create an unloving atmosphere that will undoubtedly affect one's health.

I shall never forget the couple about whom I wrote in my book *Stress and Nervous Disorders.* They were arguing with each other during a consulting hour. They were really angry, swearing at each other and telling each other in no uncertain terms what they thought. The gentleman had asked me for some help in dealing with this problem. They were on the brink of divorce and, basically, I could not see either of them bringing their behaviour to an end. I told them to go home, take a piece of paper each and write all the negatives about each other on one side and, on the other, list all the positive attributes.

It appears that the list of negatives was the length of your arm, but sadly there were only a few positives. The woman sat down and examined her list. She wanted to save her marriage so she decided to change her way of thinking and disregard both the negatives and positives. She put her list on her husband's pillow, with a note which said, 'I want to forget about the negatives and positives. I love you unconditionally and I love you with all your positives and negatives, just as I loved you when we first met.' I am happy to say that they are still together and have seen their children mature in a happy atmosphere, thanks to a few well-chosen words, which helped determine their future.

It often does not take a lot to turn a difficult situation around. Where illness and disease are concerned, we have a tendency to focus purely on the physical symptoms to find out what could be wrong, but if we don't consider things from a holistic angle also, we may never find the answer.

We may say, for instance, that arthritic and rheumatic conditions can be the result of an infection, an allergy or an unknown condition, but when we examine the emotional part of life, and we experience hate, feeling unloved, jealousy or resentment, we often see that those degenerative illnesses – including cancer – can ensue from such unhealthy emotions. It is therefore extremely important that we look holistically at the body in order to establish the trigger for any of these conditions. If we establish possible causes, then work towards improving matters, a deeper harmony and better health can be achieved by simply adjusting one's thoughts to a more positive attitude of love and peace.

While writing about this, I thought of a lady who consulted me some time ago. She was very distressed, uptight and almost gasping for breath as she tried to tell me what was wrong. As she was crying inconsolably, I gave her some *Hypericum* (*St John's Wort*). It emerged that she was consumed with anger and hatred for her husband's secretary. Although she dearly loved her husband, behind her back he had become involved with his secretary and had unfortunately fallen in love with her.

The message she received from her husband was clear – he was going to leave her for his secretary and they planned to go away together. She was so full of hatred that she could hardly tell me the story and I practically had to drag the words out of her. I then gave her some *Heather* from Dr Bach. I have always found Dr Bach's Flower Remedies to be of tremendous help in dealing with a negative state of mind. *Heather* is a hateful plant. It pushes all other plants away and wants to take over. It is also a very jealous plant. This lady was not only extremely distressed about the situation she was facing, but the fact that this secretary, as she said, was so much more attractive and younger than she was, filled her with jealousy. Bach Flower Remedies are of tremendous benefit in such instances, as their characteristics and signatures tell us for which emotion they are helpful. It was quite amazing to see how her attitude changed after she took the *Heather*, so that we could talk calmly and rationally about the problems and how best to confront them. We often notice with those plants that 'hate' and those plants that 'love' that their extracts will be of great help in overcoming life's problems in order to gain better health, peace and love.

I have learned to value nature and it is often my best adviser. It is interesting when studying plants, herbs, roots and trees to see how they grow in nature and how they survive. The Essences that I have been able to produce are the result of spending many years in defining the nature of the plant, the herb or the flower. Flower Remedies can be of great help in boosting the positive part of one's nature and can be given when it is necessary to improve certain characteristics.

I will never forget a doctor's widow from the Shetland Islands who told me that long ago they knew which plants and herbs to use by simply looking at their signatures. This lady was almost 100 years old when she spoke to me about the terrific benefits obtainable from *St John's Wort*. She said if you put it in some oil overnight, it would turn a blood-red colour, which is a clear indication that it is a wonderful remedy for blood circulation. If you examine its leaf under a microscope, you will notice hundreds of tiny holes filled with the extract of *St John's Wort*, which wants to shout out to you, 'I love you, I want to heal and help you.' It is for this reason that it was named after St John, the apostle of love.

I often think back to the time during the War when my mother's help was needed in a home for the elderly in Arnhem Oosterbeek. Next to the home was a large monastery. At a time when bombs were falling around us, I became friendly with an old monk who tended the herb garden each day. During some peaceful moments, he told me about every plant and herb, and the signs that God had given them. He told me to look at the little wood pansy, a tricoloured flower with petals like satin. As our skin could be compared to a piece of beautiful satin, this little flower tells us to 'use me for your skin'. I cannot think of anything better than *Viola tricolor* to help repair damaged skin. It is even gentle enough to use for any skin blemishes on a newborn baby.

If we take a look at how mistletoe grows up a tree, clinging like a parasite, just as cancer grows like a parasite in the human body, it is saying to us, 'I am the plant of life and death. You will find the negatives and the positives in me. I am a parasite on this tree, like cancer is a parasite in the body.' I have seen many people in my lifetime being greatly helped by the homoeopathic extract of mistletoe, *Iscador*.

If we look at the artichoke, *Cynara*, and its form, we see how it can help the liver or, in combination with *Milk Thistle*, can be used as a liver tonic. Another brilliant remedy, *Ginkgo biloba*, comes from the *ginkgo* tree, one of the world's oldest species of tree. In China, this is known as the 'memory tree' because of its action in maintaining and improving one's memory. If we examine its leaf, we notice a peaceful harmony between its two sides – a heavy leaf, almost split in half and just held together by a thin stem – a perfect example of the human brain. God gave it the signature for how it should be used – keeping positive and negative together (as in both sides of the leaf) in a spirit of harmony that can be nothing but beneficial for mind, body and soul.

'Peace' and 'love' – two words which are so necessary in today's society, two words which need a lot of exercise to enable us to experience these emotions ourselves. Doesn't it give us a good feeling to love and help the less privileged? We often like to please ourselves but in so doing we weaken ourselves and others. It is only unconditional love that can facilitate peace and harmony.

To love and to be loved is very special – and this also applies to the animal world. It is amazing to see how much love an animal gives in return for the little care it receives. Because I have treated so many horses, dogs, cats and birds during my years in practice, I have learned to understand animals more. From the famous racehorse to the little stray dog, they have taught me so much, and the terrific pleasure I get from treating animals encourages me to help as many as I can. However, my hands are tied because, by law, only vets can treat animals. As I want to keep on the right side of the law, I always ensure that the vet is aware of any treatment I am giving, or that the owner has had the vet's approval before consulting me.

I have sometimes been able to treat successfully famous racehorses where conventional veterinary care has failed. This gives me the most pleasure, especially when those horses carry on to win further races which would otherwise have been impossible. When a horse is in pain and you relieve that pain, an amazing tenderness is visible in its eyes as gratitude for the way in which you have treated it. The honest eyes of animals, such as the many dogs I have treated, always follow you around.

Even when an animal has been hurt on the road or a bird has been brought in after being hit by a car, once their pain is relieved by treatment, they exhibit this thankful expression in their eyes that I often don't get from humans. Things are frequently taken for granted in the human world. Often we forget to show a little appreciation and love for the efforts made to help human suffering. With animals, it is different – time after time they show love beyond explanation.

I have seen this often with our own dogs. I remember Tamara, a 14-year-old Samoyed we had had since she was one.

She was always very grateful for anything you did for her, and I shall never forget the day she died. We did everything possible to help her, as the whole family loved her so much and could not bear the thought of her leaving us. I well remember that morning when I said goodbye to her. Her eyes followed me wherever I went. I knew she was nearly at the end of her life and while waiting for the vet to arrive, I went back to comfort her one more time. Although she was very weak, she used all the power within her to lift her front paw as her way of giving me a last paw of thanks. It broke my heart because I knew that I had lost a very true friend. Love can sometimes be very difficult to express in words. It is often by our attitude or by the way we handle things that we show someone if we really have the capacity to love or to be kind in this often hard and cruel world.

Peace and love can easily be influenced, either negatively or positively. They are two very fragile emotions – like a love/hate relationship or a peace/discord situation. I always feel so sad when peace is disrupted by seemingly minor mis-understandings that can spiral out of control. I have seen some of my best friends' marriages and the successful marriages of others going completely wrong because of this. It is so important to communicate with each other and to try to understand or accept certain situations to maintain peace and to keep love alive in a caring relationship.

However, there have been many times during my life when I have been encouraged by patients who, in some way, wanted to show their appreciation for the little I did to help, as with a very kind gentleman from Northern Ireland who happened to be one of my very first patients. I had a good relationship with both him and his wife. They were both ill and I tried to do all I could to help them. To those people who express their love and kindness to others throughout the world, I am happy that I can give them something back. I was aware of how much this particular gentleman had done, not only for the underprivileged but also for charities and many other worthwhile causes. He was a very wealthy man and wanted those in need to share in his good fortune. I think that is the reason he was granted such a blessed life. Many times he tried to pay me more than was necessary and I always said that I did not approve of that sort of practice. I can honestly say that I am not the sort of practitioner whose aim is to make money. I have always tried to give the best to my patients and to see them as a part of myself.

Because he was determined to show his gratitude, however, unknown to me he donated £5,000 to help fund a project on complementary medicine at Queen Margaret University College. When I later learned of his generous gift, I felt again the kindness of this loving man who had done much in support of peace in Northern Ireland. Many other patients, in their own way, think of ways of giving back some of the love I have shown them.

At a lecture, a lady enquired why I worked more than 90 hours a week to help so many people, and what my purpose was in doing so. It is certainly not for money. It is because I want to help those with problems, and the lengthy waiting lists at each clinic are evidence of this need. I said to that lady that when you give love, you receive love. It is a very simple fact, but it always works. There is always a place for peace if you want it to happen, and there is always a place for a loving, kind deed to help others in this often sad world.

A newspaper reporter who interviewed me some time ago asked an unusual question: 'What is the most loving thing that you have seen during your lifetime?' I must say that I was overwhelmed by the love shown when we all suffered at my father's departure. My father had developed cancer during the War, and at a fairly young age we had to say goodbye to him for the last time in this lifetime. He was a very kind man who helped a lot of people and had a loving word for everybody. In the darkest hours during his last few weeks on this Earth, my mother, brother, sister and I were so moved by the love shown to him. When he was in pain towards the end, one member of the family stayed with him in hospital overnight. Every morning there were three pairs of clogs outside the hospital entrance (a lot of people wore clogs in Holland at that time). For weeks on end, sometimes at five, six or seven o'clock in the morning, three men my father had known throughout his life came to offer him some comfort before going to work. The loving kindness I saw from those men, who greatly valued my father's friendship over the years, was so touching that I learned what real love means.

Real love, sitting in silence with an occasional kind or loving word, can mean so much during some of the darkest hours that one endures in life. It is during such occasions that we see this immeasurable love that makes life worthwhile.

I was once asked to take over the management of a pharmacy business in The Hague for a week so that a young family could have a well-earned holiday. Because I knew this family really needed a break, I was very happy to help. One day I had to go to the post office, which is in one of the busiest parts of The Hague. I rode quickly on my bicycle, but on the way back, although I was on the correct side of the very busy road, a car struck me. I was thrown forcefully over the handlebars and landed on the pavement, sustaining a bad head wound. Some onlookers carried me into a chemist's shop. By coincidence, one of my dearest and oldest friends happened to come in shortly afterwards and he was shocked when he realised it was me who had been hurt. He dropped everything, got a taxi and took me to the nearby hospital, where I was looked after with great devotion. When I was discharged in the evening, my friend took me back to his home, where his wife cared for me and insisted I stayed. She made a lovely meal and I shall never forget the love of those two elderly people who cared for me so well. This reminded me yet again of how wonderful this world would be if love were more freely given.

Just recently, I was deeply touched to receive a beautiful card from an elderly lady I had treated. She had painted the card herself and in it she thanked me for the way I had helped her during the last 30 years. Her words were very kind. She said, 'Your help does not go unnoticed and I have found great comfort in the genuine help and care that you have always given to me. I look forward always to seeing you, and think of the words of Oscar Levant, "Happiness isn't something you experience, it's something you remember".'

Happiness can be achieved if we produce the real love and real peace that are so necessary in this selfish, commercial world in which we live.

CHAPTER NINE

My Fight for Truth, Honesty and Reality

What is truth? There is a story in St Matthew's Gospel (13:44) that I often think about in relation to that question. A man had a large field and hidden in that field was a treasure, but he had to dig for it and make every effort to find it. That treasure was the Kingdom of Heaven, which for me epitomises truth. I am fortunate to have found that little pearl, having searched for it since I was a child.

Listening to people's stories every day, I often ask myself what really is the truth. It is not easy to find. One has to search for it, and although sometimes one can easily say, 'That *is* the truth', one has to question oneself, 'Is this right?'

My struggle to find truth began when I was very young. In Holland, there are two types of schools. Education starts with kindergarten, followed by primary school and then higher education, and one has a choice of either going to a religious school where the Bible is taught or to a non-religious school. My problems started at kindergarten. Because my father was a religious man, it was decided that I should attend the Christian school where great emphasis was put on the teachings of the Bible. As I listened to the Bible stories being read, I started to challenge what the teachers were saying. When an old uncle died and I was told he was going to heaven, I questioned the existence of heaven and hell. Being an inquisitive five year old, I kept asking, until one day the headmistress suggested to my parents that it would be better if I went to a non-religious school, as she felt the questions I was asking were not really suitable for the other children to hear. The teachers probably thought I was becoming a religious freak. It was decided to transfer me to a non-religious school, which I actually enjoyed very much. I became friendly with the headmistress, who was able to provide me with a lot of answers – but only up to a point.

Then primary education started and, once more, I attended a religious school where the same problems surfaced when I started asking question after question which were never answered to my satisfaction. One day, the headmaster told a story about the battles between the Catholics and Protestants and how the Catholics burned people who did not follow the principles of being a good Catholic. He said the Protestants were better than the Catholics. I asked the headmaster why this was so, as Calvin and some religious Protestants were also burning people, and why were they fighting when everybody should believe in the same God? The headmaster became extremely angry. He told me that I was a nasty, bad boy, and how dare I attack the Church fathers who had done so much for the freedom of religion. He then put me into a dark cellar for half a day to reflect on the sins that I had committed. When I returned to school the following day, I was still not satisfied, so I badgered him again until I was sent, as punishment, to sit for the afternoon in the girls' classroom. When my mother became aware of what was going on, she luckily came to my rescue and sent me to a non-religious school.

My search continued for that treasure of truth until I realised it is actually quite straightforward. One only needs to consider a few values that the Bible puts forward simply in three principles: first, that one must worship God in spirit and in truth; second, that one has to be born again and third, that everybody has to appear before the judgement throne of God. These may appear to be three simple principles, but they will take a whole lifetime to fulfil. Christ himself explained it so anyone could understand by saying that 'if one had the face of a child, it would be given to them'. When I recognised those three simple truths, a bright light shone. I have often spoken about the power of that light which will be experienced even more during prayer and meditation, a power that is bestowed on Man that he can use to great advantage. In my book *Female Cancers*, I wrote about some incredible case histories of people who had experienced that light and, through that light, how much healing they had been able to achieve, to the extent that some were even able to reverse their conditions. Once that light is discovered, life will take on a totally different meaning and, by following the second principle, 'to be born again', this re-creation will emerge as a new creature who will be a part of that great Universe that God has created for Man, if he accepts it.

The first thing that God created was light, but that was a spiritual light. If we discover that light and walk in that light, then we have a part in the almighty power that God will give to Man to keep him in contact with the great powers that He will freely give to Man during his existence on Earth. A new creature, a new creation in one's life then takes over, which has so much more meaning and is so powerful that truth can then be experienced by everyone if there is a willingness to accept it.

I have experienced many misunderstandings during my life, especially when I chose the lonely road of alternative medicine. I remember once giving a lecture on the truth of homoeopathy and the misunderstandings and the misinterpretations that were prevalent. Everyone is entitled to his own opinion, but when all those opinions have been put forward, it is advisable to then ask yourself, 'What is the truth of the matter?' or 'What is truth?' In the end, it all boils down to reaching exactly the same acceptance as Samuel Hahnemann, the founder of homoeopathy, achieved hundreds of years ago.

Making an issue of the question 'What is truth?' can be very interesting. If one takes the trouble to discover the truth, no matter how small the issue, a very positive outcome can be reached. It is worthwhile taking the time to look into such matters and to realise that, if we make an effort, the truth can be found, just like the man working hard digging in the field to find that treasure. The treasure of truth in one's faith is without doubt the most valuable commodity that one can inherit in this life. It becomes part of an eternal life in the spirit that can continue to live in a different world where problems, difficulties and disease can be conquered.

When I was thinking about this, it reminded me of a boy of about 18 years old who lost the use of everything below the eighth dorsal vertebra in a car accident. Nevertheless, he had a strong determination to get better. The mind being stronger than the body, he put every effort into this and I helped him as best I could with counselling and homoeopathic remedies. Some feeling returned, as luckily everything was not totally destroyed. He was in a wheelchair after the accident, but because of his strong belief that he would get better, he managed to heal himself.

When he went to his specialist and said he had some feeling back in his legs, the specialist crushed his hopes by saying that he should stop dreaming, as it would be impossible for him to get better. He asked the consultant if that was the truth. The consultant said, more or less, that it was. The young man then said he had evidence that some life had returned to his legs, which had not been there previously. The specialist shrugged his shoulders.

It is very important that one always tells the truth. If that specialist was not completely sure – which obviously he wasn't – then he should have said to his patient that if he had some feeling there, then they would work on it to try to improve matters. When I see patients are putting every effort into helping themselves, I tell them to give it a chance and work on it, but without giving them false hopes. Praying and meditating and clearly visualising themselves as being well again will be most beneficial. The result for this young man was that he improved over time and is now walking unaided.

The power of truth and the power of faith can be strong enough to exercise the body to obey. It is extremely important that we look at the situation as it really is. One of my very best friends, who is a wonderful homoeopath, gave me a small extract from a book that her father, M.H. Abrams, wrote in 1953, entitled *The Mirror and The Lamp*. It gives an insight into 'the matter of truth' from every angle. He writes:

> Of special interest to us are writers who, like Keats, contrast the poetic and scientific descriptions of a natural object, but use the instance to demonstrate that the two outlooks are compatible and mutually invulnerable. In a passage which Keats probably remembered while writing Lamia, Hazlitt admitted that, as a matter of historical fact, 'it cannot be concealed' that the progress of knowledge and experimental philosophy 'has a tendency to circumscribe the limits of the imagination and to clip the wings of poetry', yet, he added, scientific and poetic observations are not exclusive alternatives.

His example is of a glow-worm, which the naturalist carries home to find that it is 'nothing but a little grey worm'. The poet visits it in the evening when:

it has to build itself a palace of emerald light. This is also one part of nature, one appearance which the glow-worm presents, and not the least interesting; so is poetry one part of the history of the human mind, though it is neither science nor philosophy.

Leigh Hunt preferred the lily as his example:

> Poetry begins where matter of fact or of science ceases to be merely such, and to exhibit a further truth; that is to say, the connexion it has with the world of emotion, and its power to produce imaginative pleasure. Inquiring of a gardener, for instance, what flower it is that we see yonder, he answers 'a lily'. This is a matter of fact. The botanist pronounces it to be the order of 'Hexandria Monogynia'. That is a matter of science . . .
>
> The plant and flower of light, says Ben Jonson; and poetry then shows us the beauty of the flower in all its mystery and splendour.

I would merely add that I find it difficult always to express myself as I would wish. I love truth with all the simplicity of my heart, to be my all, the light to help and to shine for all time, which is a matter of truth.

It is that truth which will turn honesty into a reality, because as soon as that truth is found, then honesty becomes a very important part of life. Honesty will always win over dishonesty and although justice sometimes seems far away, the truth of the matter is that honesty will always win. If one twists the truth, then dishonesty will result. It is quite interesting to see that the spirit of honesty follows those people who have been honest in life and, in the end, it always pays to tell the truth.

I remember some 50 years ago being visited by two tax officers in the town where I was brought up. They wanted to inspect our pharmacies' books, and we welcomed them because we were quite sure all our records were in order. While chatting to these inspectors, one asked from which de Vries family I came. I told him that my father and grandfather had been in the tobacco industry, and the inspector said he knew them well. The older of the two gentlemen mentioned my grandfather by name and asked if my father was Hendrik de Vries, which I confirmed. Even in those days there was strict control over tobacco and tobacco tax. He told me that they never found it necessary to inspect my grandfather's business, because they felt he was the most honest man in town and everything was always perfectly in order when they carried out any small checks. He felt sure I would handle things in a similar vein. I agreed that I had to live up to the high standards of the family, being well aware that they had strong principles and that they did everything possible to keep a clear conscience. The outcome was that our business was in order and I was advised that no one would inspect any of our other premises.

Honesty will always pay and having a clear conscience helps to ensure a good night's sleep. I meet many patients suffering from insomnia, which often results from not having a clear conscience. This reminds me of a story that another great friend once told me, which he narrates as follows:

This is a story of a man who had a qualification. His qualification was, 'I can sleep on a windy night.' The background of this was that, in mid-western America, farmers used to hire labourers by the season – summer or winter. A particular farmer and his wife went to town on the day when the hiring took place, but as it was rather late when they arrived, nearly everybody had been hired and the town was becoming deserted. But as they walked the streets, they saw someone leaning at a corner, and they asked him if he was looking for work. The man replied, 'Yes, sir.' 'What have you done on a farm?' the farmer asked. The man answered, 'I have done all the kinds of work there is, sir.' The farmer then asked what qualifications he had and what he specialised in. The man replied, 'My qualification, sir, is that I can sleep on a windy night.' The farmer further asked, 'Yes, and what else?' 'Any job on the farm, sir, but that is my qualification,' the man replied. So the farmer and his wife walked down the street and wondered what he meant by that, as they did not think it was much of a qualification for a farm worker. However, as he was the only person there, and no one else could be found, they went back and told the man that they would hire him. They took the labourer back to their home and got him settled in. He lived with the farmer, ate with him and worked with him. He had his own little room at the top of one of the barns, where he went every night to be out of the way. He got up in the morning to milk the cows, and did all he was asked. Everything went well. But then one night, in the middle of the night, a terrific storm arose and the wind was howling and the rain was lashing down, so much so that the noise woke the farmer and his wife. The farmer sat up in bed and said, 'I wonder if everything is all right.' His wife wondered if the hen coops were all shuttered and if the sacks of corn and the sides of the barn were properly sheeted down; she also wondered if the door of the pigsty was wedged, because the pigs could easily push through it. The farmer said that he would get up and go and have a look. So he got up and inspected the whole place with his lantern and found everything in apple pie order: the sheets covering the corn were all held down with huge stones, there were wedges behind the pigsty door and the chicken coops were all well fastened and bolted. As everything was all right, he returned to bed with a peaceful mind. When they were having breakfast the following morning, the farmer said to the labourer, 'That was a terrible storm last night.' 'Oh, was it – why, what happened?' asked the labourer. 'Oh, the wind was terrible, so I went out to check everything.' The labourer asked if he had found everything to be in order, to which the farmer replied that everything was perfect. 'Well, sir, I did tell you that I can sleep on a windy night,' replied the labourer.

The moral of that story, of course, is that as the labourer did his job with honesty and was reliable, his clear conscience enabled him to sleep soundly.

It is important to realise that honesty follows when one exercises truth. I have seen this very plainly in the 50 years that I have worked in the field of medicine. There are, as I have said in the previous chapter, some medical people who shake their heads or shrug their shoulders and say quite firmly, 'We don't know enough about it, so we will leave it alone', or there are those who are dishonest and say, 'There is absolutely nothing in it. I don't know anything about it, but I would suggest that you don't give it a chance.'

I was very encouraged the other day when a patient told me that his doctor had sent him to our dispensary for *Linoforce*, which is probably one of the finest remedies for constipation. It was produced by Alfred Vogel and I have worked with it for an exceptionally long time. Apparently, this doctor had difficulty himself with constipation and had been advised to take this product, with great success. Because he had experienced that it worked he had no hesitation in recommending to his patient that he take *Linoforce*, saying it would help him greatly. That is being honest, and the evidence of the truth that it worked for him made him share this fact, as he knew it would also help his patients.

A patient told me a story recently of a time when he was in hospital. The consultant examined him thoroughly and advised him on several methods that might help him. The patient said that he already followed those methods, having been advised by me to do so, adding he did not expect the consultant would approve of Jan de Vries. The specialist looked at him and said, 'Look at that book. We catalogue a lot of his case histories because of his great successes. We record in that book what he has been doing and, when it is justified, we recommend our patients try his methods.' That is being honest. For the benefit of patients, we need to work together to make them better. I like that sort of spirit. It is not only a question of being honest but also of working for the well-being of patients. It is of no benefit giving patients false hopes whatever treatment they are receiving. The truth is that reality will speak.

Whilst writing this particular chapter, a patient handed me something that he had written about himself. I read it and decided to include it here because I know this gentleman as being an honest, truthful and admirable person. In his writing, he tells about 'That Other Way' he found to conquer his problems:

> One year past in September, I was dumped when I was told by a local doctor that what I had lost, I had lost. I had suffered with a bad chest for some six years, having developed asthma, and the situation was becoming more chronic by the day. By this time I was on four inhalers that were not meeting the need and my war cry for a few years had been the phlegm that most sufferers know of only too well. My outlook was dismal to say the least and it seemed like the death knell had rung over me. I was in a very poor state of health and losing weight every day owing to constant sickness due to the phlegm.

Just about that time three people unknown to each other were serving me with the same advice, 'Why don't you try Mr de Vries?' My prospects for better health were very slim and in my mind I had nothing to lose, so I accepted the three-cornered advice as confirmation that I was meant to contact this gentleman in Troon. I did so and the date was coincidentally made for the very next day. 'There was another way' and I was about to give it a try.

I will never forget my first consultation, which offered me hope and confidence. Mr de Vries said confidently, 'I will make you a new man!' I freely admit that the first few months were really tough going and I began to wonder what was happening to me. However, in the back of my mind there was a mental picture of a lady from Devon walking the hills who had been as I was, but after about 18 months on the treatment was a changed woman. 'If he can do it for her,' I said to myself, 'he can do it for me.' By March, I began to feel myself turning the corner. I hasten to add that I was still attending my own doctor and visiting a chest specialist in the hospital and there were antibiotics and steroids but the outcome was that I was reduced from four inhalers down to one and, in the summer, I was discharged from the chest clinic as 'stabilised'. The hospital knew that I had visited Mr de Vries but sadly treated the matter as by the way. I don't think they took 'that other way' seriously. Thirteen months later, I am still on one inhaler; no more wheezing or breathlessness, the phlegm problem greatly reduced; no more sickness due to phlegm; I have put back about a stone in weight; look a lot healthier and have a sense of well-being that I haven't had in years.

In the event of passing on the good news, it is like preaching the gospel to the unconverted; I wonder in amazement at the unbelief of others in spite of the fact that my recovery and well-being is obvious. So many people are in a mind-set, conditioned by a wrong attitude and prevalent scepticism. There is another way. To the unbeliever, all I can say is that, 'whereas I was plagued by chest problems, today I am that new man! There is life after inhalers.'

That patient experienced the reality. I much prefer patients to be honest when they consult me. Over the years I have worked in Scotland, I have come to realise that the Scots are generally honest enough to tell me whether or not they will follow a particular diet or plan. Sadly, there are a lot of people who say they will do it and then don't, hoping that they will get better on their own. The patient who wrote that passage followed my instructions to the letter and consequently reaped the benefits.

Belief becomes very powerful and one becomes a new being when illness and disease have been conquered. So what is the reality of the matter? I am aware that if you break a leg or you have a burst appendix, then hospital treatment is required. The battle between orthodox and alternative medicine has been tremendous over the years. Misunderstandings, misconceptions, lies and all kinds of things have played a role in the fight to prove the efficacy of what is now termed 'complementary medicine'. The reality of it all is that many people who have taken the orthodox route and have not been satisfied with the results have found success when they subsequently followed the alternative system.

It is crucial that honesty should be shown to patients by hospitals. I admire those doctors, nurses and hospital staff who devote their lives to the well-being of their patients. The reality is that we should all be grateful for the research work that has been carried out over the years and practised at university and other hospitals, and to honour that with appreciation. But then there is the reality that, in alternative medicine, so much research work has been ignored over the years, and the many doctors and professors who have been sceptical and have not given it a chance or a proper trial have squandered so much in the fight to relieve human suffering.

When I think of the indispensable machinery and instruments that are used today in alternative medicine to discover illnesses and diseases that were overlooked by orthodox methods, one can only be grateful that there was a school of thought that contradicted the orthodox system when questions were left unanswered, meaning that people could seek help from alternative methods and receive the treatment they needed.

I realise I was probably labelled as being a difficult and sometimes nasty little boy at school for asking questions. Even now, at my age, I still keep asking questions. I know there is not always an answer for everything, but one has to strive for it – one has to work, to dig and to plough in order to find an answer whenever possible.

If we look at the great discoverers in the world, the effort they have put in and the many times they have failed, we realise they could quite easily have given up. Instead, they left no stone unturned in trying to find answers. Because of their determination, we all benefit today from their hard work. Everyone should be grateful that those people who were classed as being 'difficult' have been a great blessing to others. That is the reality of it all.

How often do we get things out of context? Sitting down, thinking about it, then going back to find the truth of a particular matter often makes us realise how wrong we have been. Sometimes when my children were growing up they would make up some fantastic stories that obviously had no truth in them, and I would say, 'Please do get real.' Getting to grips with a situation is often very difficult, but it is so important. Yes, we have to get real and get organised in our minds to find out the importance of a particular subject.

These three subjects – truth, honesty and reality – make one think.

The reality is that alternative medicine is gradually becoming complementary medicine. During the last 50 years, I have striven to have the two systems of orthodox and alternative medicine working alongside one another. We still encounter many bigoted people who think 'there is no substance to it' and, unfortunately, this is the same on both sides of medicine. The truth is that nowadays we cannot manage without orthodox medicine but neither can we manage without alternative medicine. That is why we talk about complementary medicine, where the two systems can be used in conjunction to help human suffering.

I once met a wise elderly doctor, who said that it doesn't matter what system one uses, as long as it is of benefit to the patient. When patients cry out for help, it makes no difference what method they follow, as long as it helps them out of a bad situation. They deserve to get better if that can be achieved, and that is what we all strive for. We are here in life for only a short time and we want to enjoy it fully, but there are sometimes conditions that are beyond our control and, in such instances, one has to learn to face up to the facts and accept the inevitable, but not before taking every course of action possible to try to help the particular condition.

During the years that I have been in Scotland, I have heard too often of people giving up without a fight and thinking they cannot improve a situation. I am not a great believer in that attitude. I feel that when there is a problem, one has to do everything one can to solve it and not to give in by thinking, 'I will never get better.' Surprisingly, once we discover how powerful the mind and body really are, and the help that is available in trying to overcome a seemingly unbeatable situation, the outcome in reality can become something entirely different.

It is imperative to look for the right treatment. Over the years, I have seen the benefits achieved by homoeopathic methods, as well as other routes that have been taken such as osteopathy, naturopathy and acupuncture. It is essential to find qualified people who have the scientific knowledge. I find it most encouraging that the forefathers of alternative medicine had a very commonsense view – and let me say, there is nothing common about common sense – of their treatments and the application thereof.

Some newspaper journalists nowadays report that alternative medicine is something new, and write lengthy articles boasting of great discoveries that have been made. It must be emphasised that alternative medicine is older than orthodox medicine. It has been with us for a long time and it was brought to the fore by the pioneers for its acceptance as far back as 100 years ago. I have certainly pioneered for the acceptance of alternative medicine, not only in Holland but also in Britain, but I would never say that I was the discoverer of these treatments. The treatments have been practised around the world for generations and, particularly acupuncture, as far back as five or six thousand years! The success of a practitioner depends very much on gaining as much knowledge as possible in a specialised field and discovering what it is all about. If that is achieved, the success will be evident in the waiting room.

One day, an enthusiastic practitioner, full of good intentions, sat in front of me crying. He was young and so desperate to have a thriving practice, as I have seen with many others over the years. He told me that he had tried everything he could to attract patients and had even introduced a lot of other treatments, some of which probably had very little in common with what he had been trained to do and, indeed, some could even have been classed as gimmicks. I advised him to go back to basics with the treatment that he had learned, to concentrate on that and to give 100 per cent to his patients by putting his heart and soul into the work he was trained for. He would then probably become more successful. When I saw him again a few weeks later, he told me he was already seeing the benefits of my suggestions.

The reality of orthodox medicine and complementary medicine still remains – if we stick to what we know and we put 100 per cent into it, we will be successful. After all, we can only do our very best. Whichever treatment is decided upon – whether orthodox or alternative – it is there to help alleviate human suffering.

CHAPTER TEN

My Fight for Compassion

During the 50 years that I have worked diligently to give my very best to my patients, I have felt extremely guilty that, in so doing, I have often neglected my own family. Although I did all I could, the time I spent with my daughters while they were growing up was fairly limited because of the long hours I dedicated to my work. I realise how much I missed out on, not being able to devote more time to them at that important stage in their lives. Nevertheless, we are luckily gifted with ten wonderful grandchildren, with whom I try to spend more time, although, because of my exceptionally busy life, this is still something about which I feel guilty. However, I was so moved when a well-known magazine interviewed one of my daughters who is a successful businesswoman. The interviewer asked all kinds of questions. When asked what her husband had done for her, she said that he had taught her to be correct, accurate and tidy. Then he said, 'I believe that you are the daughter of Jan de Vries.' When she said she was, he said, 'I would really like to know what your father taught you.' Her simple answer was 'Compassion.'

When I read that article, I felt it a tribute to me and was really thankful because I have always believed that one of the most important aspects of life is our ability to show compassion. So often ruthless decisions are made without a thought for others, and many people can be harsh and show no understanding at all. It is always good to be able to exercise compassion, especially with people who are ill or who feel they have come to the end of the road. So I felt very content when I read that article. Although I still feel guilty about not giving my children the time they deserved while they were growing up, I have always tried to be a good example to them.

When I was around 18 years old and still busy studying, I was already taking my first step in helping people by working with an elderly professor in the nearby hospital. He donated all his consultation fees to the hospital as one way of showing his gratitude for the years he had been hidden there in the War as, being Jewish, the Nazis would have tried to capture him. A small man, with a long white beard, he had eyes as sharp as an eagle's and an incredible brain. He was one of the most eccentric people I have ever met but he had tremendous knowledge and many brilliant ideas in his approach to treating patients. Although his methods were basically very orthodox, he had introduced all kinds of homoeopathic and herbal ideas into his practice.

I recollect a lady who came in with a nasty-looking

suppurating wound on her arm. She had been advised that her arm would have to be amputated. I will never forget the way he put snake poison into the festering wound and prescribed several homoeopathic remedies. It was miraculous how that wound healed.

People streamed in to see him with their various problems and a consultation session that should only have lasted an afternoon sometimes continued late into the night. It was quite incredible how he managed to carry out this difficult job. Witnessing this gifted man at work and learning from all his ideas and his vast experience offered me a golden opportunity, although all I was really asked to do was bring people in and out and give him whatever he needed. He treated people in a truly sympathetic way, which was almost unique, and I learned a lot about compassion from him.

I learned to exercise compassion very young, not only from my parents, who were extremely kind-hearted, but also when I lost my little school friend who died of cancer. I visited her every day to keep her company when she was suffering dreadfully from this monstrous disease. Following her death, another good friend needed a lot of care when he was stricken with polio. I took the task upon myself of helping him get to and from school each day and looking after his needs there.

I became even busier when I was about 18 when an elderly, crippled lady fell off the bus in front of me and broke her arm. I tried to ease her pain before she was taken to hospital and visited her when she returned to her old people's home. She was really a lonely soul and extremely grateful for my help. I realised that I was possibly the only human company she had and she became quite insistent that I visit her every Sunday afternoon, which I did, although I admit that I never expected that my free time would be as severely restricted as it was for the next few years by those weekly visits and by carrying out errands and other tasks.

By this time I had learned quite a lot about the vast subject of compassion. On my way to visit this elderly lady one day, I witnessed an attack by a ferocious dog on a tiny kitten. There, before my eyes, the dog savagely killed the kitten and then strolled off. Its owner never even scolded it, so I took the liberty of speaking to him. I told him I was deeply concerned that he had allowed his dog to viciously kill that defenceless little kitten. He shouted at me to mind my own business. I was extremely upset and felt something needed to be done to stop such a thing from happening again. I sought out the local animal protection society and became extremely active, helping animals and raising funds. We were able to open a home for mistreated animals in our town, which had an operating room and a local vet to do all the necessary work. I was pleased to be involved because I felt I had to do something worthwhile to protect the lives of neglected animals.

After I graduated and moved to a small village where we had our pharmacy shops, I continued in my crusade, raising money to open our own homes to protect animals. In this country village I again witnessed many heart-rending deeds. When kittens were born, I saw to my great sorrow how farmers put them into weighted bags and drowned them. It seemed to me that the farmers were heartless in destroying the litters, particularly as they liked to have cats around their homes. Here I became a committee member of the animal protection society, campaigned for regulations against such cruelty and opened a special unit to care for newborn kittens so that they would not have to face such an appalling death. Although this kept me extremely busy, I enjoyed the work and I have been pleased to treat animals where I can ever since.

When looking after my own animals, I could see that they suffered pain in the same way as humans. However, humans can describe their symptoms. It can be frustrating when dealing with animals because they cannot tell you what is wrong. I remember when one of my pigeons had a stone in its throat and it looked helplessly at me. I phoned the local vet, but as he was very busy I had no option but to operate on it myself and remove the stone. That was the only surgical operation I have performed in my life. All this took place on my kitchen table, and the pigeon went on to live for many more years.

We used to have French bulldogs, and kept the first two born in the litter. One was called Adam and the other, Bobo. They were lovely, extremely affectionate dogs and were very close to the family. However, Bobo had problems and the vet decided that a hysterectomy was necessary. I have never seen such a pathetic-looking little dog as Bobo after her operation, which had affected her emotionally to such an extent that she required great care and attention.

Compassion is a very strange thing, especially where animals are concerned. It is so rewarding when you are given such thankful looks by an animal in return for the help you offer. I saw that clearly with my Samoyed, Tamara, whom I have already mentioned. Samoyeds, often called 'the laughing dogs', are lovely animals, but before she came to us at one year old she had been mistreated and must have endured much hardship, which meant she initially displayed a nasty streak in her character. My second daughter, Janyn, worked incredibly hard with her and, with a lot of loving care and attention, she developed into a wonderful dog. We went through a lot with that dog, but she was very strong and even survived a parvovirus infection. I became fond of Tamara and I will never forget the months of suffering I endured after we lost her. I have written of Tamara's last moments with us in Chapter Eight. I was so upset when she passed away, and I have never witnessed such thankfulness from an animal in rewarding me for what I had done for her. I was so moved when we buried her. Unfortunately her son, Raja, had managed to get out and looked on from a distance. Raja instinctively did not come near Tamara as he normally would have done. Some people believe that animals have no feelings or that they don't understand, but they do – and often to a greater extent than humans.

Here is a story of compassion that is very difficult for me to analyse, as I was extremely fond of my father. He suffered the after-effects of the torture that he sustained during the Second World War, and when he came to the end of the road, he suffered terribly – much more than Tamara did. His agony lasted for a long time and we all prayed for his departure to free him from pain. The paradox of the story with Tamara and my father is that it is very difficult to explain compassion. We were all relieved when my father found release from his suffering. Although I suffered for months following the loss of Tamara, it seems hard to believe that I never shed one tear when my father left us. We were a close-knit family and very fond of each other, but there was such a difference in the way I coped with these two situations.

What is compassion and where do we apply it? I thought of the following story, which may make it a little clearer.

Last year an old lady was murdered outside a Glasgow tenement. The story interested me for the simple reason that there were five passers-by who witnessed this brutal attack but no one stopped to help. There was a lot of media coverage surrounding this murder as the police tried to piece together what had happened and asked for witnesses to come forward. When I read that five people had passed by and had not tried to help this elderly lady, it was obvious to me that there was a total lack of compassion. It seemed that three of those witnesses were afraid to do anything purely because they did not want a brush with the law, another one was frightened of the attacker and the fifth said he hadn't noticed what had happened. Law and order are vital, but the law needs to be changed if people are too frightened to become involved in incidents for fear of doing something wrong. It is for this reason that the old motto 'to love thy neighbour as thyself' is rapidly disappearing. It is distressing to think that people have become so blasé about compassion and friendship that being selfish and having an 'I am all right Jack' attitude has come very much to the fore. I have seen this in my own country of

Holland. The pre-war people were very loving, compassionate and understanding. However, after the euphoria at the end of the War passed, I clearly saw this change in spirit to 'as long as I am all right'. Today, when I visit Holland I am ashamed of that attitude and of the aggressive and brutal behaviour that I encounter there. In my mind, I often blamed this on the young people, but I now sometimes wonder if today's society is responsible for cementing this sort of selfish attitude in their minds. If law-abiding people have come to the stage that they cannot be bothered to help their fellow human beings for fear of having a brush with the law – as I think they have – then isn't it time for a radical change? We have to examine and review this kind of attitude and ask ourselves, 'Where will this all end?' Life is very special when we learn that life means sharing.

Loneliness is probably one of the worst illnesses in the world and can lead to enormous problems. With the sort of selfish attitude that is becoming more prevalent today, the situation will eventually arise when little compassion is left, leaving individuals feeling extremely alone. This does not only affect those from less privileged backgrounds but also the most affluent in our society. This became apparent to me one evening when I was asked to go to a palace in London to see a young crown prince from another country. His father and mother were probably the richest people on Earth and were very keen that I saw their son, who, in time, would be educated to take over from his father and rule their large country. I spoke to this young fellow on my own for a short while. Although he was only about seven years old, it became obvious that his problems stemmed from loneliness, misunderstanding and missing the love that he desperately needed. Even with seven men in attendance to see to his every need, I could see that this little fellow needed some close monitoring, to experience some normal living and to be guided as to what life was really about. As I looked at him, I was full of compassion because, although he was a nice chap, he was well on his way to becoming totally disobedient. His slight hyperactivity needed control by dietary management and he needed some commonsense education. I took on the job of looking after him. I spoke to his nannies and left a message for his parents to say that if they really wanted to make something of this young boy, then he needed to gain some sound understanding of life. Luckily, the message was understood and now he is much better. The importance of that story is that compassion is not only needed when there is real trauma, but also in simple situations which, if left untreated, could get completely out of hand.

Both my wife, who used to work in education, and I tried our best to teach our children the real meaning of love and compassion. In their work today and in their daily lives I am very happy to see that they have exercised this in every possible way and have been of great help to many people.

My mind goes back many years ago to a nice hotel in Lochearnhead, Perthshire, called The Four Seasons, where we spent some special family time together. We stayed in one of the houses in its grounds and had meals in the hotel. When we were out for a walk one day, I saw an elderly gentleman having a nasty fall. I went as quickly as I could to help, but my four daughters – although small at that time – reached him before me. I was very touched to see the love and compassion they showed this elderly gentleman so that, by the time I reached him, they had already done all that was necessary. I was delighted that they were practising what they had learnt at home.

Small children in distress deserve great care and compassion. One day a lady came to see me with a young child. Weeping, she told me that while she was pregnant, her husband had been shot dead and that her parents lived far away. When the baby was born, it had uncontrollable fits and was diagnosed as being epileptic. The poor child had been prescribed all kinds of drugs, but these had not had a significant effect. The mother was at the end of her tether. I laid the baby on my bench and looked at this perfect example of Creation. As I watched, she had a fit and I decided to work on her immediately. I asked if she had been born by Caesarean, which she had. That started me thinking. I was certain that the terrible trauma experienced by this baby while still in its mother's womb, followed by being brought into this world by Caesarean section, must have had some bearing on those uncontrollable fits.

When I began some cranial work on her little head, I discovered some slight damage, which had resulted in the fits. Her little eyes looked up at me as if pleading for help and she looked so insecure. She was a lovely baby and she let me work on her without crying. When I finally found where the problem was in the cranium, it only took two seconds to make the necessary adjustment, and a miracle happened – that baby never had a fit again. The mother was so grateful that this small correction was all that was necessary to improve the quality of her baby's life. It is reassuring to realise that often something can be done when one feels, like this mother, that there is nowhere to turn. It is often a question of being in the right place at the right time. I saw the girl again when she grew up, and I still see her mother who remains grateful for what I did for her daughter, who is the joy of her life.

While writing this chapter, I recalled a horse that stood 17 hands high. It was a lovely beast that had won many prizes, but it had become wild and uncontrollable. The owner cared deeply for the horse but feared it would have to be put down if nothing could be done. She said it had developed a sort of Jekyll and Hyde side to its nature after two things happened. First, it had become jealous when a pony encroached on its territory, as it had been accustomed to getting the attention. Second, it had developed allergies. Tests showed that the horse's dietary management needed to be changed, and, using iridology, I discovered that its nervous system needed drastic attention to achieve a positive result. I managed to change its attitude by giving it a few homoeopathic and herbal remedies and, by transforming its diet completely, it slowly returned to its normal self. The horse lived happily for quite a few years and even went on to win some important races. The negativity of a situation can often be overcome by showing compassion and by making necessary lifestyle changes.

Life can be much more fulfilling when there is compassion. To explain this a little further, I call to mind a case where endless compassion was necessary when a young man was reaching out for help. One evening, just as I was ready to leave after an extremely busy clinic, a worried father phoned me about his son, who was in a dreadful state. The father was a hospital consultant but did not know where to turn next. His son had been a very capable student who had already progressed quite far towards his PhD and was looking forward to a bright future. Sadly, this all came to an end when something happened that escalated into a chronic situation. The father begged me to go to see his son. As I was leaving the country the following day, I resolved to go there and then, and asked a friend if he could drive me.

When we arrived at their home, we found an extremely concerned father and mother. I listened as they told me how their son, once with such a promising future, now lay in a darkened room as he could not tolerate daylight. Nobody could offer any explanation other than that he was suffering from severe ME (myalgic encephalomyelitis). ME is often very misunderstood by the medical profession, so his parents had had a difficult time getting his problems recognised. They told me that their hard-working son had had a busy social life and a lovely girlfriend, but, a few months before developing these health problems, she had ended their relationship. He had then become quite depressed and more and more withdrawn. As a result, his work suffered and he became so tired and drained that he had no other choice but to return home to be looked after by his parents.

I was asked to see him in his room, but as it was in complete darkness it was impossible for me to carry out any iridology to establish what could possibly be wrong. He did not even have enough strength to talk. As he lay there, I checked his pulse, which was extremely weak. I spoke to him calmly and asked him if I could feel his throat and the lymph glands under his arms, which indeed were all very swollen. I managed to find out a bit about his medical history, and felt that a lot of compassion and time were needed to help this poor fellow. As I have so often said, Man has three bodies – a physical, a mental and an emotional body – and certainly with this young man, all three were in great disharmony. I promised I would soon return and, for months on end, I visited him in this dark room with its windows blackened out. I gradually made some headway in helping his condition. It was a very slow path and a lot of compassion was necessary to get him through the process.

After thorough detoxification and much counselling, he started to become accustomed to a little light. By that time, he was managing to eat some fruit and had become slightly more communicative.

His parents had also mentioned that he suffered from aggressive mood swings. I witnessed this for myself when I was having one of my regular deep conversations with him one evening. He was feeling very tired, as he had been out that day, and had found the light unbearable. He became very angry when I said something that touched a raw nerve. He suddenly stood up, slapped my face, punched me and then fell onto his bed crying. I remained calm and compassionate, and I think he felt ashamed of his behaviour. I then told him in no uncertain terms what his problem was and that we had to deal with it. When he was able to get that anger out of his system, I saw him slowly but surely improving, and today he is back to normal. Sometimes it needs a great deal of patience and understanding, but, above all, endless compassion is needed to understand human suffering.

On a lighter note, however, one has to be careful where and how to be compassionate. During my early days working with Alfred Vogel in Switzerland, his beautiful little house, with his laboratories, was home to my studies. In the third part of my autobiography, I will talk at greater length about my life and work with Alfred Vogel and describe more fully his home and the laboratories. Everyone who worked there was extremely industrious. My wife and I also worked very hard, clocking in at 7 a.m. and often clocking out at 8 p.m. There were few laws to regulate working hours, particularly in that region of Switzerland, and the Swiss took their work very seriously. As the controls and inspections of this type of work were of the highest standard, no one could afford to make even the smallest mistake.

My assistant was a 72-year-old lady. She was very diligent. Before she started work at 7 a.m. she milked a cow and then had to walk through the forest for an hour to get to Teufen where, on a steep hillside, she finally reached her workplace. She was a great help to me but, because of her age, I was concerned about her. I felt compassionate towards her, and I sometimes gave her some extra francs when she went home for the weekend, as she had told me how poor she was. She invited us to her home one Sunday afternoon. My wife and I walked to her little farmhouse and, when we went inside, we were shocked at what lay before us. Placed on the stone floor was a wooden chair, a wooden table and an uncomfortable straw bed – that was all she had. While we were joining her in a cup of tea, her young grandson came in, and we again felt moved by the plight of these hard-working people. At night, she walked us home in the dark, helped along the way by her little lantern, and then she returned to her bare farmhouse where we had left a small gift of money for her and her grandson. We felt full of compassion for their situation. We respected the hard work and help of this elderly lady who, although always friendly towards us, was quite reserved.

I decided to have a word with the laboratory manager, who was a personal friend of Alfred Vogel, to try to get a little bit more money for her by providing extra work that she obviously desperately wanted. He started to smile and asked if I had given her some money. I said I had. He then told me that while both he and Alfred Vogel might be considered quite rich, their combined fortunes were overshadowed by the money this 'poor' woman had. He pointed out the land and the farms that she owned and yet she lived in a world where she felt she could not spend one penny in improving her own or her family's situation. He told me it was a typical attitude of the elderly, reserved, conservative Swiss, who believed that they were poorer than the poor and had to live in this way to safeguard their inheritance. It was a revelation to me when I heard that story, which was later confirmed by Vogel himself, who told me that she would not even let him use any of her land for growing herbs. Instead of hoarding her money, she could have been using it to enhance her life and that of her family, thereby enjoying what had been entrusted to her.

This cautionary tale reminds us to ensure that help is given where it is really needed. It is necessary to be aware of the full facts.

I am never too tired to raise money. I have managed to raise hundreds of thousands of pounds for many charities during my life and I am aware that, when I do so, the money will go to where it is really needed. We have to show compassion by supporting the needy and sharing with them a positive vision of the future in this increasingly selfish world.

CHAPTER ELEVEN

My Fight for Vision

It was in 1958 that, during my first visit to the beautiful city of Edinburgh, I found myself at the corner of Royal Terrace, clutching a bouquet of flowers for my host and hostess. As I stood, viewing the panorama of the city, I asked myself, 'What am I going to make of my life?' I did have a vision, however, and that vision was wholly focused on giving the public the freedom to choose which medicines or treatments they received – by offering them a natural alternative.

It has been a bitter fight during those years, and one that has often led to great misunderstandings as when, in 1961, I was threatened with imprisonment if I refused to stop practising natural medicine. In those days, it was seen as 'quackery', and you lost all your friends if you went into that field of medicine. I stood there pondering what would face me along the difficult road I had chosen – a lonely, yet fulfilling path. The idea of helping people who had been told by orthodox medicine that there was no hope greatly interested me. This was not solely because of the help I could give them but because of my great concern as a pharmacist at witnessing the number of new drugs flooding the market. I wanted to find a way of making people aware of the unwanted side effects attributable to these drugs. On that particular Saturday, I made my way to Hillside Crescent to be with my hosts, the Youngs, whose only son, Charlie, a navigator, had been shot down over Holland during the bitter fighting of the Second World War and whose grave I had had the honour to tend.

At supper the following day, my future was mapped out for me in that rich tapestry of life, ensuring that I would spend most of my life in my beloved Scotland – I met the girl who was to become my wife. Things moved rapidly from that moment and we became engaged in 1959. However, I once more became aware of the lonely path I had chosen, as the girl I was to marry had no time for alternative medicine. Again, I had to fight for understanding but fortunately I won. We got married in 1960 and, although she was still not keen on my chosen career, she stood by me and has helped me through what were some very difficult years.

My vision for the future was to fulfil the promise I had made on the tram tracks in Arnhem Oosterbeek during the brutal Second World War. Viewing the devastation of Operation Market Garden, after the horrific destruction of Hitler's bombardment which had cost so many young lives, I promised God that I would devote my life to helping other people if my mother and I were fortunate enough to survive. Seeing the destruction and death, I developed a deep desire in my young heart to help people in need wherever I could and to fight for peace, for life and for something with more value than all that could be destroyed in one moment.

Although I have always done my best to help people, I am saddened when I look around today and see how little people have learnt from that terrible war, and I ask myself, 'How can we find permanent peace? How can we stop terrorism and war?' The answer is that we can only put a stop to them if we all wake up and visualise ourselves as being part of the world that our Creator laid out so beautifully for us. We have a duty to protect His Creation. We must realise that there is only one answer to this terrible, divided, uncivilised world where terrorism and war have caused such misery. If we want to take peace into our own hands, then we have to show by example how strongly each individual is prepared to work in this way to gain peace.

We are all aware of the horrific events of 11 September 2001 when terrorists hijacked four US planes, killing nearly 3,000 people in a matter of hours – a disaster which caused many people to despair for the future, not realising that destroyers will be destroyed. We get out of life what we put into it. With that simple thought in one's mind, there is only one solution – every person will be rewarded for the kind of work he or she does. That terrible disaster still speaks to us as a memorial to innocent victims whose lives were sacrificed when evil took over.

A very good friend of mine worked in one of the buildings totally destroyed. After a few days, trembling and in fear, I phoned her and was so relieved when I heard her voice. Why was she saved? Only God knows. The day before this disaster struck, she had terrible toothache and made an appointment to see the dentist the following morning. Her life was saved by that dental appointment. She thought of all the friends she had lost and she asked God, 'Why was I saved?' Was it coincidence or was she saved to work for humanity? She experienced the same feeling that I had on the day following Operation Market Garden when I was just a young boy.

It is possible to achieve peace if we all realise the formula: although each individual is only a drop in the ocean, we all belong to that ocean and everybody in that ocean has a place to fill with a love for peace and understanding. This can only come from the heart. There is no government that can truly protect against the heartless brutality of terrorism. It is sad to think that many of the monuments that have been erected throughout the world are reminders of evil deeds. Taking matters into one's own hands can never achieve peace. It can only be accomplished if everybody has a desire for peace and, by striving to achieve it with a vision that everything will become new, by God's great love, Man will one day be able to enjoy a peaceful world in a search to find that wonderful light that I spoke about earlier – to become a child of the light and to spread that wonderful message of truth, honesty and reality.

Although I often have had battles on my hands, time after time I have been encouraged by my vision to help others. I recollect the wonderful experience I had when a young doctor, Dr Sarah Marr, came into my clinic. She was very charming and I could see that she had a caring heart. She had sustained dreadful neck problems following an accident. She had really come to me as a last resort as she didn't have much faith in alternative medicine, but she had gained no benefit from other treatments. Fortunately, I was able to help her recover using acupuncture. Her mind was then open to the value of alternative medicine, having personally experienced the benefits. She adapted her totally orthodox practice and it was with the greatest pleasure that I went to work with her in Ravenswood, Glasgow. During those few years, we both witnessed the benefits people gained from a combined practice – which we shall call 'complementary' – with so many obtaining relief from their different ailments.

We once went to a research meeting in one of Glasgow's hospitals and listened to the different opinions being voiced on disease. When we came out, we agreed that both orthodox and alternative practitioners had a lot to learn. We were both open-minded enough to recognise that one cannot be bigoted where medicine is concerned. It is an untapped field where much can be learnt and where there is a need for understanding to develop the tools to make this world a better place. When we worked together I would often reiterate, 'Sarah, we still have a lot to learn,' and after being in this field of medicine for 50 years, I am still of the same opinion. Because we both had that desire, her Ravenswood practice became a haven for many people and today I regularly hear from those we were able to help.

I encountered the same experience in the Elmfield Group Practice in Gosforth, Newcastle, where five doctors worked together in the orthodox field while I was the only one in the alternative field. Most of those doctors were honest enough to admit that they knew nothing about alternative medicine but were willing to learn. When a newly qualified doctor joined the practice and saw the fusion of orthodox and alternative treatments, she asked the senior partner, 'What is this all about?' The senior partner replied, 'Look and see for yourself.' This young doctor and I developed a wonderful working relationship by uniting to help people in need, and we learned so much from each other – that is what it is all about. We were all totally aware that we were there to help alleviate human suffering. I had a wonderful few years there and realised again what it meant to help people who were searching for ways to alleviate their distress.

Do we exercise the vision we need to help each other? Do we really understand what it takes to have that vision which is so pertinently expressed in the Bible, 'where there is no vision, the people must perish', by learning to understand each other and by helping, even without the other person realising what we are doing?

I recall the speech my Dutch friend, Dr Hans Moolenburgh, prepared for my youngest daughter's wedding. Mhairi and her husband, Marcus, both work in the field of medicine and he wanted to encourage them. He told them that although they had this difficult calling and had a great amount of professional knowledge, there was something that was more necessary. He started by explaining that he had known many medical professors who knew so much that they had become 'top-heavy and tumbled over' and yet were poor healers. On the other hand, he had known many humble therapists, who perhaps had only a little knowledge but, one after another, people were healed. He concluded that nowadays we do not really have the right idea of what is needed to help our sick fellow human beings for, whilst knowledge is necessary, there is that other imponderable that enters the equation: Therapist + Patient = Help. He said that the best way to explain this was by recounting an old story about two brothers:

> Long ago, there lived in the Middle East two brothers. They were both farmers and they were also neighbours. One brother was married and had seven children, and the other brother was unmarried. In those times, long ago, that meant that you hadn't children either. Just after their wheat harvest, the unmarried brother could not sleep. 'Here I am,' he thought, 'with all that wheat, and there is my brother with eight more mouths to feed. I'll give him some extra wheat.' So he filled two bags with wheat and, in the dark night, staggered to the barn of his brother to deliver the bags. In the meantime, the married brother could not sleep either and thought, 'There is my poor, unmarried brother who has to go through life all alone. I will compensate his loneliness by giving him some extra wheat.' So, in the middle of the night, he staggered to the barn of his brother and delivered two

bags there. Much astonished were both brothers when they discovered next morning that the amount of wheat had remained the same. They both thought that they had merely dreamt their good deeds, so that night they stayed awake and repeated their performance. Again, the amount of wheat had not diminished. So, on the third night, they took their bags and looked carefully around on their way to the other man's barn. So it happened that they bumped into each other on the border at their farmyards. They straight away understood what had happened, dropped their bags and fell into each other's arms, crying, 'Brother'. At that very moment, the Lord looked down from heaven and said, 'That is the way I meant people to behave towards each other. On that place, I will build my temple!' That happened where Jerusalem now is.

This complete and unconditional goodwill towards each other is the real ingredient of healing. Healers and practitioners need, apart from their knowledge, that basic love – not the love that says, 'If you scratch my back, I'll scratch yours', but the unconditional love known as 'agape' in the Bible. One cannot just whistle this up – one has to work for it and do one's very best to perform it in life.

One has to have a vision. I am tremendously encouraged by our own Queen Beatrix in Holland. She, like her mother, has done so much to strive for peace in this world. Although she is aware of the circumstances throughout the world, in her speeches she advises the nation to look forward, and not to be bigoted, but to have a vision. I often think back to the time she was crowned, when she was asked which king or queen she admired most. Without hesitation, she immediately said it was King David from the Bible who tried to lead very difficult people but admitted his mistakes and was prepared to learn from them. He too had a vision for the future and a vision of God's great Creation, writing those wonderful Psalms to remind us of his enormous ability to work for peace and understanding but, above all, for the love of his Creator. Queen Beatrix, through some of her difficulties, has shown that her vision for the future is quite clear. She has lived with the people and is a great example to them all.

Before my grandmother said goodbye for the last time, she warned the family to keep a lookout, as the selfishness in the world would grow and grow. We live in a very selfish world, where it is often a case of 'I am all right Jack' and where we forget to love our neighbours as much as ourselves. That is important for the future. It is a sad fact of life, though, that some people learn this the hard way. The positive spirit that was so evident following the Second World War, when people displayed a willingness to work together towards peace and to prevent war breaking out again, seems far away nowadays. To work selflessly to fulfil that vision which is so dear to us may mean sacrificing material possessions in order to achieve improved economic situations.

I clearly recollect, on the day following my graduation, receiving a letter from the largest drug producer in Holland. A meeting was arranged and they offered me an excellent position, with the prospect of a wonderful future, and at the time I considered accepting the job. I was shown around the factory and saw the drugs that were produced there. However, when I came to the department where the animal experiments were carried out and I saw what happened to these innocent creatures in order to create more drugs, I asked one simple question of the man who interviewed me: 'If that is what happens to animals, what will happen to human beings if we pump so many of these drugs into them – could we turn them into zombies?' I realised I could not be part of that picture and, although it was a difficult decision (because I knew I would have had a bright future there), I decided to return to what became – especially in the beginning – my lonely path. Now I am so thankful that alternative medicine is receiving the recognition it so rightly deserves by being part of a complementary system that is extremely necessary.

I was president of the London and Counties Society of Physiologists during 1997–9. Because of my busy workload, I am sure that I wasn't one of their best presidents, but I enjoyed my years of service, being in contact with people who had one desire through their work – to help people in need. I met quite a number of the several thousand members, and they all possessed that united spirit which encouraged them to help relieve human suffering. I saw that same spirit among the committee members. Their founders had a vision, but the strongest vision came from Ken and Audrey Woodward, whom I mentioned earlier in relation to the Northern Institute of Massage. I admired and respected their diligent efforts to make that vision become a reality and their devotion to their hands-on work in educating people who sought proper training. They worked tirelessly to make this Society stand out, and they succeeded, because they had one clear view in mind: to help others. Whatever we do and wherever we are heading in this uphill struggle in life, we should establish a good foundation by visualising ourselves as giving our very best.

Not everyone's thought on vision is the same. We all have individual visions, as I learnt just a few Saturdays ago when a strikingly attractive young woman sat in front of me. She was probably in her 20s, and although she looked very healthy, she wanted to discuss a few minor problems with me. I looked at her and then glanced at her name on the piece of paper that lay before me. I said to her, 'Before we start dealing with your problems, you should know you were the best healer before you were born of anybody I know.'

Her eyes looked at me in bewilderment and she asked what I meant, so I explained what a wonderful healer she had been to her mother. I clearly remember the day her mother sat in front of me, gasping for breath. One of her lungs had collapsed, the other lung had a hole in it and she had great difficulty in breathing. It looked as though there was no hope of recovery. I asked her what her greatest problem was – whether it was purely her breathing or if there were other things troubling her. She said, 'Believe it or not, in my condition, I have also become pregnant.' I was extremely worried about her and told her that all I could do to help was to prescribe some *Echinaforce* from Alfred Vogel, which would possibly keep her clear of further infections. I also advised her to carry out the well-known Hara breathing exercises that I teach and, as many people will know from his book, *Living Proof: A Medical Mutiny*, were of tremendous help to Dr Michael Gearin-Tosh. I told her to discuss the situation with her doctor but not to forget to do the breathing exercises. She was to contact me if there was anything further I could do.

A week later, she and her husband came to see. They told me that her doctor and the specialists had advised an abortion. This idea was completely against her principles, and she asked if I thought there was any chance she could make it through her pregnancy, as she dearly wanted a baby. I looked at her again, thought of the situation she was in and told her that it was not up to the doctor, the specialist or me to advise. It all depended on her own vision on the matter – the final decision should be made between her husband and herself. Her husband then said, 'Then there will be no abortion.'

The doctor in question contacted me and told me that we had to persuade her to have an abortion to save her from a lot of misery. I told him that although this might be his vision, the decision was entirely up to the prospective parents. The couple sought further reassurance that things would be all right. Again I told them that they must follow their own instinct on the matter. They decided to continue with the pregnancy and she asked me if I could see her regularly, which I did. To my great surprise, her health continued to improve. Of course, as most people know, encephalins and endorphins are released during pregnancy, which enabled her suffering to be eased. As time passed, with the mother-to-be's health improved and the baby progressing well, I wondered how she would cope during labour. She did everything she could to prepare, putting a lot of effort into her breathing exercises, which greatly improved matters. This method of Hara breathing has been a blessing to so many people throughout the world when practised in the way I teach. Thankfully, any fears I may have had about the birth were unfounded. A very healthy baby girl was born and that baby had cured the mother.

Nature will always overrule science. Science said, 'Here is an impossible situation,' and the answer was abortion. Nature said, 'Please give me a chance,' and it showed once more that nature overrules Man's scientific thoughts on the matter. I thanked God when I looked at this beautiful young woman sitting before me, who had been an amazing healer in her mother's womb. I could not help thinking again how remarkable vision really is, and that it is good to follow a vision with a mind that belongs to nature, as we need to obey the laws of nature and, in so doing, obey the laws of God.

I often think of another young girl who came to me following a horrific train accident. During this ordeal, her life flashed through her mind – her childhood, her family and her grandparents – as she thought this was the end. She had wanted to marry and have children, so as the train derailed and she saw it heading towards a tree, she focused her mind on stopping it. When the train eventually came to rest, a flow of energy suddenly entered her body. She felt that God had come to tell her that her life had been saved and she had been given this boost in energy for a reason. She looked around at the devastation, where even the table in front of her had collapsed, and the air was thick with dust and debris. Bodies had been thrown around in the two carriages in front of her, yet nothing appeared to be wrong with her at that moment. She was filled with this great love and a strong desire to offer help and compassion to her fellow passengers, which she did. As she often rationalised that event in her life, she said she was conscious that her guardian angel had been looking after her and, when she learnt that so many people had been killed in the front carriage, she often reflected on her miraculous escape. As she said, that experience was necessary to make her value life and to make her realise how quickly it can all be taken from us. It had freed her from all selfishness, as she so beautifully described it to me.

My friend Hans Moolenburgh told another story at my daughter's wedding about his favourite aunt, Corrie ten Boom. A lot of people have probably read her writings, but there is a great lesson to be learnt from the story that she told him personally. In Haarlem in Holland, the city where Hans works, there was a watchmaker's family who hid persecuted Jews during the War. In the end, they were betrayed, and two sisters, Corrie and Betsie, were taken to the concentration camp in Ravensbrück. There was a very cruel female guard there and, through her bad treatment, Betsie died. Corrie was miraculously released and, after the War, she gave a series of lectures in German. One day, a woman came up to her after a lecture and said, 'I've done terrible things during the War, but recently I have become a Christian and sought forgiveness for my misdeeds, but the Lord has said to me, "I will only forgive you when one of your former victims forgives you." Will you please forgive me?' Straight away, Corrie recognised that cruel guard and stood rooted to the ground. She simply was not able to do it.

Then she remembered that in the Lord's Prayer it says, '*Forgive us our trespasses, as we forgive those who trespass against us.*' Our sins cannot be forgiven when we do not forgive others. So, not because she felt anything, but because she obeyed the scriptures, she put out her hand and said, 'I forgive you, sister,' and only after she had acted in that way was she flushed with real compassion for the woman.

This is closely related to healing. Never ever think that we, as practitioners, can heal. It is always a smile from heaven. The only thing we have to do is to plant the healing seed; the rest is not our doing. Those patients who are not cured give us the necessary humility. For ourselves, we are nothing, and I have never ever said that I have cured anybody. Many times I have said, 'God cures, I only try to heal.' In that spirit, I have carried out my work now for 50 years, in the knowledge that I simply want to be guided by the only One who gives and takes life. It is comforting to think that I have been able to help many people. Yet we have to realise that it is only because of a gift that has been entrusted to us that we are enabled to help others.

Often, when we emerge from the dark experiences in life, we conclude that it has all been worth it. Also, we see individuals who have been helped to lead full lives once more, when those lives had almost come to an end, become more compassionate people – often because of their experiences. Such experiences serve as a reminder to us all to appreciate how fragile life is.

Following a morning clinic, my spirits were low after seeing so many discouraged patients who had been told they only had a short while to live. That afternoon, I had to give a lecture in a place that was almost packed to the ceiling, and I asked myself, 'How many people are there who need help?' Although I was quite disheartened, there are always people who can sense the right time to offer encouragement to move forward. A lady in the audience wrote me a little note, and she commented that when she saw all those people giving me their undivided attention, she wondered how I kept going at my age and how one small head could carry all that information. That is probably the secret of it all: knowing that we are one small drop in the ocean, yet so much can be entrusted to us to enable us to help others less fortunate than ourselves.

In coming to the end of this book, when I bring to mind the 50 years that have passed, when my life has been used to help others, I have one great desire – and that is to do even better, to work for something that is worthwhile, to try to steer away from the selfishness and the evil that surrounds today's world, and to realise that one can only stop this by taking into one's hands what is good and by enriching one's life by that which is light. Light has no communication with darkness. Once that great light is entrusted to us, and we walk in that light, we can become a shining example.

BY APPOINTMENT ONLY SERIES

Arthritis, Rheumatism and Psoriasis	ISBN 1 84018 558 9	£5.99
Asthma and Bronchitis	ISBN 1 84018 554 6	£5.99
Cancer and Leukaemia	ISBN 1 84018 555 4	£5.99
Heart and Blood Circulatory Problems	ISBN 1 84018 553 8	£5.99
Life Without Arthritis – The Maori Way	ISBN 1 84018 966 5	£5.99
Migraine and Epilepsy	ISBN 1 85158 820 5	£5.99
Neck and Back Problems	ISBN 1 84018 556 2	£5.99
New Developments for MS Sufferers	ISBN 1 84018 464 7	£5.99
Realistic Weight Control	ISBN 1 84018 559 7	£5.99
Skin Diseases	ISBN 1 84018 561 9	£5.99
Stomach and Bowel Disorders	ISBN 1 84018 952 5	£5.99
Stress and Nervous Disorders	ISBN 1 84018 829 4	£5.99
Traditional Home and Herbal Remedies	ISBN 1 84018 937 1	£5.99
Viruses, Allergies and the Immune System	ISBN 1 84018 564 3	£5.99

NATURE'S GIFT SERIES

Body Energy	ISBN 1 85158 267 3	£5.99
Food	ISBN 1 84018 628 3	£5.99

WELL WOMAN SERIES

JAN DE VRIES HEALTHCARE SERIES